THIRSTING FOR GOD

THIRSTING FOR GOD

A Yearbook of
Prayers, Meditations, and Anecdotes

MOTHER TERESA

Compiled by Fr. Angelo Scolozzi, M.C.III.O.

CHARIS

SERVANT PUBLICATIONS
ANN ARBOR, MICHIGAN

Charis Books is an imprint of Servant Publications especially designed to
serve Roman Catholics.

Servant Publications
P.O. Box 8617
Ann Arbor, MI 48107

Cover design: Paul Higdon
Front cover photograph: FPG International LLC. Used by permission
Back cover photograph: UPI/Corbis–Bettmann. Used by permission

00 01 02 03 10 9 8 7 6 5 4 3 2 1

Printed in the United States of America
ISBN 1-56955-227-4

LIBRARY OF CONGRESS CATALOGING-IN-PUBLICATION DATA

Teresa, Mother, 1910-1997
Thirsting for God : Mother Teresa's yearbook of prayers, meditations,
anecdotes, for the third millennium / Mother Teresa : compiled by Ange
Scolozzi.
    p.   cm.
ISBN 1-56955-161-8 (alk. paper)
1. Church year meditations.   2. Catholic Church Prayer-books and devo-
tions—English.   I. Devananda, Angelo.   II. Title.
BX2170.C55T48   1999   99-33943
242'.2—dc21   CIP

I thirst.
JOHN 19:28

Only one secret:
The closer we come to Jesus,
the better we will know his thirst.
MOTHER TERESA, M.C.

Blessed are they who hunger and thirst for
righteousness, for they will be satisfied.
MATTHEW 5:6, NAB

DEDICATION

To Bishop Joseph A. Galante, who accepted from
Mother Teresa, M.C., the legacy of the Missionaries of
Charity Third Order, M.C.III.O., as a seed of new
evangelization for his diocese of Beaumont, Texas,
and for the church.

To Sister Nirmala, M.C., Mother's worthy successor.

To the parishioners of St. Mary's, Cleveland, Texas,
who for two years allowed me to be a servant of communion among them.

And to the countless co-workers of Mother Teresa,
M.C., around the world, who have now become like a
new "Diaspora," a free movement of love and service.

With an admiring, grateful heart,

Fr. Angelo, M.C.III.O.

Acknowledgments

Heartfelt thanks to Pat Jennings, who tirelessly
typed and retyped the manuscript so many times.
Without her help and encouragement I would
not have been able to pull it all together.

Diocese of Beaumont
Office of the Bishop
P. O. Box 3948
Beaumont, Texas 77704-3948
(409) 838-0451/735-7187
Fax (409) 838-4511

PRESENTATION

Thirsting for God
A yearbook of prayer and meditations
by Mother Teresa M.C.

As we are about to enter the new millenium Father Angelo Scolozzi, M.C.III.O. has put together ***Thirsting for God,*** a year book of prayers and meditations by Mother Teresa. This book is a reminder to us to look always for the basics of our faith: prayer, the value of each human being and a recommitment to the Gospel.

My prayer as this book is published is that it will be an instrument to continue to spread the deep and vibrant love for Jesus and the earnest concern for all people which so characterized Mother Teresa.

Signed at the Diocese of Beaumont
April 22, 1999

+ Joseph A. Galante

Most Rev. Joseph A. Galante, D.D., J.C.D.
Bishop of Beaumont

PROLOGUE

Every successful person is driven by a vision, a call, and only the ones moved passionately become realized individuals within their lifetime.

Mother Teresa, M.C., was one of these souls! We read in the Bible, Psalm 42:3 "My soul is thirsting for God." She indeed was parched by this thirst.

A psychiatrist from the United States came years ago to Calcutta wanting to write a book about success, and wanted to interview two people living there: Mr. Birla, one of the richest men in India, and Mother Teresa, M.C. His interview consisted of a single question: What is the secret of your success?

I do not know what the answer of Mr. Birla was, but Mother Teresa said, "Jesus' thirst: Love others as God loves you."

Toward the very end of her life she wrote a special message "I Thirst" to the whole Missionaries of Charity Society. I quote from the manuscript: "Only one secret. The closer we come to Jesus, the better we will know his thirst."

To quench Jesus' thirst was the purpose for founding her religious society. This particular "call within a call" she received during the now famous train ride to Darjeeling at the foot of the Himalayan Mountains on September 10, 1947.

This day, known as Inspiration Day, is currently celebrated by the entire Missionaries of Charity Society.

The first printed draft of the "Constitutions of the Society of the Missionary Sisters of Charity of Calcutta, Marian Year 1954," Part 1, Chapter 1 states:

"The general aim of the Society is to quench
the thirst of Jesus Christ on the cross for
love of souls."

This prompting made Mother Teresa, M.C., who she was and motivated her throughout her life to do the things she did. The morning of her death, September 5, 1997, in her last general letter, which she left unsigned, she wrote:

"September 10 is coming very close, and that is another beautiful chance for us to stand near Our Lady to listen to the thirst of Jesus and answer with our whole heart."

Since my first contact with Mother Teresa I have had no other desire than to put my footsteps on the ones she made as she followed Jesus. Truly from my infancy, I had been longing to have an idea of the love that one would feel in the presence of Mary the Mother of Jesus. I felt this flow of loving goodness when I first glimpsed Mother Teresa in 1976 at Calcutta's mother house. I was waiting in a small courtyard and saw her approaching between the gray buildings, bare feet and white sari with blue border. She passed through a beam of light and suddenly I understood; my longing was fulfilled.

I remember thinking to myself at that particular moment of grace, "How good it is to be good. I will do anything to have some of this goodness for my life." I knew that only a true master possessing wisdom and holiness could pass it on to the disciples, and I was eager to learn at Mother Teresa's school of charity.

Although I had not yet fully grasped it, my life at the time was hindered by a secret wound. At the beginning of my teen years I had been molested by a religious school teacher and this episode had left a deep sense of vulnerability entrenched in my life, leaving me totally powerless to help myself.

When I met Mother Teresa I firmly believed that she would help me to find solutions to this problem and so to recover and to heal. Mother did not take the consequences of my abuse away, but by her words and example during my twenty-one years of association with her, she showed me the royal way of the cross.

Periodically she encouraged and urged me to do many heroic acts of total surrender, loving trust, and acceptance. I have not yet learned to do them with the childlike spontaneity and joy she wanted me to, but I have persevered at her school. In spite of my resistance, she invited me again and again to abandonment and to confidence to the point of harshness, of hurting. So strongly she believed that Jesus' words in the Gospel were true, and that if I remained open and willing, with faith, prayer, and penance, they would come to be realized in my life, too.

Thirsting for God is a kind of yearlong spiritual diary, a gathering of reflections, meditations, prayers, and my personal recollections of Mother. I did my best to bring back some of the unforgettable experiences of her life when she was so special yet so down-to-earth—so motherly.

My earliest editing with Servant Publications in 1985, of the first teachings of Mother Teresa, was a gift to her on the occasion of her "Jay Jayanti" (seventy-fifth birthday). Since that time a host of authors have done their share of publishing Mother's words, and today it is almost impossible to sort out all of this printed material, its origin, its authenticity, its uniqueness.

For my part, many of the stories I am presenting in this book are personal and not to be found anywhere else. I have roughly followed the pattern of the Roman liturgical calendar, putting quotes related to feasts of Jesus, Mary, and the saints at the corresponding day when it was feasible.

The sense of the liturgical year was not strong with Mother, who rather followed a path of devotion. I have tried to combine both calendar and spontaneity to give a fresher hint of her spiritual experience along with her teachings. In doing this I have availed myself of a manuscript composed by the senior sisters of the first group for renewal. They put it together as a gift of daily readings to Mother, and

Mother had passed it on to me for the brotherhood.

I have selected extracts of these materials which were addressed to and originally destined solely for the use of the sisters. I have added to it new material in a way that would make it meaningful to lay persons, keeping in mind particularly the needs of the co-workers and of the members of my own community, the Missionaries of Charity Third Order.

I have questioned myself many times during the composition of this yearbook about how much lay-people today can identify with the ideal proposed by this text. Undeniably Mother's spiritual reality was and is one of an undivided love for Christ, consecrated by the evangelical counsels of poverty, chastity, obedience, and a special fourth vow of wholehearted free service to the poorest of the poor.

Mother, in her desire to give glory to God and for the good of many souls, would have wanted to offer her ideal of consecration to anyone ready to listen. The invitation to perfection in the gospel is "To anyone who has ears to hear, let him hear!" (Mt 11:15).

In the epilogue of this book, the Statutes of the Third Order are offered to anyone interested in knowing more about this particular branch, "a new form of evangelical life," which Mother Teresa, M.C., strove to put together to the very end of her life.

Article I of the Statutes of the Third Order defines what the entity is about. "The Third Order of the Missionaries of Charity (Universal Fraternity of the

Word) is a private association of Christian faithful and a movement of new evangelization which has the same aim and spirit as the Missionaries of Charity."

The Third Order was founded by Mother Teresa, M.C., and completes her missionary work by offering to the laity the opportunity to share in the task of the "New Evangelization" of the world's spiritually poorest of the poor at the approach of the third millennium. The gospel needs to be spread, the poor need to be evangelized, yet to follow Mother Teresa is a free choice.

In the Beatitudes, which according to Mahatma Gandhi are at the core of the gospel message, we read: "Happy are those who hunger and thirst for what is right; they shall be satisfied" (Mt 5:6).

My hope is that this passionate drive which has moved Mother Teresa, M.C., to the threshold of sainthood would inspire and guide many of us at the entrance of this new millennium.

Fr. Angelo Scolozzi, M.C.III.O.
Servant Leader of Communion for
The Third Order of the Missionaries of Charity

Let us begin this New Year with a resolution. Be all for Jesus and with Jesus and you will be happy and holy throughout the year. Give yourselves over to prayer and close union with God and to a deep, joyful charity. Be a true follower of God in thought, word, and deed: if you do this in your family, it will overflow to all.

Let each of us make one strong resolution: "I will not commit a single venial sin against charity this year."

JANUARY 2

Let us make this a year of peace in a very particular way: We will try to talk more with God and to God and less with men and to men. And then, from the silence of our hearts, we can preach the peace of Christ as he did, by going about doing good to others.

January 3

Our charism is to satiate the thirst of Jesus for love of souls by working at the salvation and sanctification of the poorest of the poor. Nothing different, nothing else.

Only the thirst of Jesus, hearing it, feeling it, answering it with all your heart, will keep the Society* alive after Mother leaves you.

If this is your life, you will be all right. Even when Mother leaves you, Jesus' thirst will never leave you. Jesus thirsting in the poor you will have with you always.

*In this book, when Mother Teresa uses the word "Society," she is referring to The Missionaries of Charity: M.C. Society.

January 4

The apostles devoted themselves to prayer and to the ministry of the word. Their example teaches us that the more we receive in silent prayer, the more we can give in our active life. Therefore, on the streets, in the slums, at work, in the home, we should pray with our whole heart and soul.

We must keep that silence which Jesus kept for thirty years at Nazareth. Even now, he keeps it in the tabernacle, silently making intercession for us.

JANUARY 5

From a letter written by Mother Teresa to her confessor, Fr. Celeste Van Exem, S.J., from Entally Convent, Calcutta, 1947:

I came to India solely with the hope of saving many souls and to gain a martyr's palm. The work I have been doing all these years [as a teacher in Loreto's convent] has helped a lot to fulfill this desire. And now, last year, God came with another call within a call [to serve the poorest of the poor in the slums]. It has grown so strong, so bright, with every Mass and Holy Communion, I wonder often at his ways.

JANUARY 6

Somebody asked me: "When will poverty be over?" I replied, I believe that poverty will be over when you and I share of ourselves, of what we have and what we are. Let us give until it hurts.

JANUARY 7

Spiritual life begins with a good and sincere confession. Why confession? It is necessary for us to be free. If we are hiding or controlled by sin, we cannot be free. Sin is like a chain. It destroys life. Confession is as important to Jesus as it is to us. It is a joint action ... Jesus and me.

JANUARY 8

In the Eucharist, Jesus the Son of God is present in the form of bread. Humility doesn't mean that you hide what God has given you. Humility is truth, humility is sincerity, it is poverty and the freedom that poverty brings. Humility is woven together from these elements. If you are really humble, if you realize how small you are, how much you need God, then you cannot fail.

From Mother's diary of 1948: Motijhil.* The children were already waiting for me at the foot of the bridge. There were forty-one, much cleaner. Those who were not clean I gave a good wash at the water tank. We had catechism after the first lesson on hygiene, then reading. I laughed a good many times as I had never taught little children before.

We used the ground instead of a blackboard. Everybody was delighted, and after the needlework class we went to visit the sick. We were called into a Muslim para (Muslim home) to see a child and an old woman. We visited also a Hindu family: the mother is dying of T.B. (tuberculosis). They asked me to go often and see her. I came home early to be able to do some writing.

*Motijhil is a slum surrounding Mother Teresa's former convent of Loreto Entally, where she was a teacher before leaving to pursue her Missionaries of Charity call to serve the poorest of the poor.

January 10

Every human being has a longing for God. Christians go one step further—not only do we long for God but we have the treasure of his presence always with us. We also have the joy of getting even closer to him by receiving him in Communion. Yet Jesus was not satisfied with just becoming the Bread of Life, he also made himself the hungry one in the distressing disguise of the poor. We Missionaries of Charity cannot say that we love Jesus only in the Eucharist—naturally, we want to put that love into action, serving the poor. We cannot separate the Eucharist and the poor.

January 11

Eleven days have already gone this year. The days will go very fast. Let us not forget how Mary set out in haste in the hill country of Judea to visit her cousin Elizabeth. God chose Mary because she was full of grace and yet so full of humility. The coming of Jesus into her life generated within her great zeal and charity—zeal to bring Jesus to others through works of charity.

When the fullness of grace became one with the Word of God in her, the fruit of that union was Mary's service of love to her neighbor. She didn't dwell on the Son of God within her or on the joy and sorrow that were to be hers as the Mother of God and men.

We will be the happiest people in the world if we belong to God, if we place ourselves at his disposal, if we let him use us as he pleases.

To be this happy, we must belong to Jesus fully without reservation. He alone is worthy of our love and our total surrender. Once we really belong to him then he is free to use us, to do with us whatever he pleases.

I thirst. Hear your own name, not just once—if you listen with your heart, you will hear, you will understand.

Jesus' thirst hidden in the distressing disguise of the poorest of the poor. This thirst is a reality. He thirsts, I quench.

JANUARY 14

Ask yourself: Is your love free? Is there total surrender to God in your life? Loving trust and total surrender complete each other. Jesus had unshakable trust in his Father. In the Garden of Gethsemane, Jesus prayed: "Father, if it is your will, take this cup from me; yet not my will but yours be done." On Calvary, Jesus prayed: "Father, forgive them."

This trust was the fruit of Jesus' intimate knowledge and love of the Father. Jesus trusted his whole life and his mission into the hands of his Father. That is loving trust. Do we have that trust?

JANUARY 15

Christo Prem Prachanta: Preach to us of Christ's Love. This is what the poor people are asking from us.

A Hindu gentleman came to our house for the dying destitute in Calcutta. I was washing the sores of a sick person. He watched me and said, "Your religion must be true if it helps you to do this." I did not have to tell him I was doing it to Jesus, the action was enough. He came to the conclusion that to be able to do this we must be convinced of our call.

I am touching Christ, I am serving him, I believe that the broken person is he. Faith is love in action, not in feelings.

In each of our lives, Jesus comes as the Bread of Life—to be eaten, to be consumed by us. This is how he loves us. Then Jesus comes in our human life as the hungry one, the other, hoping to be fed by the love of our heart, by the service of our hands.

Doing so, we prove that we have been created in the image and likeness of God. God is love, and when we love we are like God. This is what Jesus meant when he said, "Be perfect as your Father is perfect."

Our duty is to satisfy the thirst of Jesus by laboring for the conversion and sanctification of souls in the slums. Our Lord chose the apostles in order to make them fishers of men, bringing many to salvation. Scripture says that we did not choose him, he chose us. He calls us to go forth and bear fruit and this fruit should remain.

JANUARY 18

Chastity touches God himself, it is undivided love for God alone. Nothing and nobody can draw us away from him.

If you have failed to be chaste, confess it now and be finished with it. God's mercy is greater than your sin. Don't be afraid, scrupulous, or anxious. You are a sinner full of sin when you go to confession, and when you come out, you are a sinner without sin.

JANUARY 19

We depend solely on Divine Providence. We don't accept government grants, we don't accept church donations, we don't accept salaries. We have consecrated our lives to the poorest of the poor, giving wholehearted and free service, the joy of being loved. People are longing to be loved, and we have the tenderness, the love of God, that continually dares.

JANUARY 20

Give yourselves unswervingly to God. Conform yourselves in all things to his glory, to his holy will. Prompt, simple, blind, cheerful obedience to God is the proof of faith.

If God loves a cheerful giver, how much more does he not love an obedient giver? We must obey with our whole heart and soul, like Jesus. He obeyed unto death, even death on the cross.

January 21

The reason for our existence is to quench the thirst of Jesus Christ. When he asked for water, the soldier gave him vinegar to drink—but his thirst was for love, for souls, for you and me.

January 22

We must all grow in a clear conviction of our duty to be holy as Jesus is holy. Holiness is one of the most beautiful gifts a human heart can offer to God.

We should serve Jesus in his poor by doing for them the things we would like to do for him. This is where sanctity is hidden for us: In knowing Jesus, in loving Jesus, and in serving Jesus in the people around us. If we do this, we will become professionals in holiness.

January 23

Joy is prayer. Joy is strength. Joy is love. Joy is a net by which we catch souls. God loves a cheerful giver: We give most when we give with joy. If you have difficulties in your daily life, accept them with joy, with a big smile! In this, others will see your good works and glorify the Father.

The best way to show your gratitude to God and to people is to accept everything with joy. A joyful heart is the normal result of a heart burning with love.

JANUARY 24

In the Gospels, Zacchaeus was a little man who wanted to see Jesus. He tried in many ways but he could not see him until he accepted that he was small. That acceptance led him to the next step, the acceptance of the humiliation that he had to climb a tree so that he could see Jesus and so let everyone know that he was very small. We need the same kind of humility for us.

JANUARY 25

We must be like St. Paul. Once he realized Jesus' love for him, he no longer cared about anything else. He didn't care whether he was scourged or put in prison. Only one thing was important to him: Jesus Christ.

Jesus the Son of God was sent by his Father to proclaim the Good News. He was fully confident that his Father would work out his plan of salvation in spite of the apparent failure of his mission. He was confident even when he saw that people did not accept him. For thirty years in Nazareth, they knew him only as the son of Joseph and Mary. Our Lady and Joseph, too, must have wondered.

People told him that he was mad, a liar; they slapped him, spat at him, and crucified him. He seemed to be a complete failure. He knew, though, that in spite of all this the will of his Father would be fulfilled. Do we have that trust?

Find at least one good point in the other person and build from there. In the family, you should thank each other, mentioning the good you have seen others do. In short, an understanding love—a love that sees the good in others—will be our goal.

JANUARY 28

The first step to holiness is to will it. St. Thomas Aquinas said: "Sanctity consists in nothing else but firm resolve, the heroic act of a soul abandoning herself to God. By an upright will, we love God, we choose God, we run toward God, we reach him, we possess him." This strong will transforms me into the image of God and makes me like him.

JANUARY 29

From Mother's diary of 1949:

Today, my God, what a torture of loneliness.

I wonder how long will my heart suffer this. Fr. Bauwins, S.J., the parish priest of St. Teresa's, came to bless the house.* Tears rolled and rolled. Everyone sees my weakness. My God, give me courage now to fight self and the temper. Let me not draw back from the sacrifice I have made of my free choice and conviction. Immaculate Heart of my mother, have pity on thy child. For the love of thee, I want to live and die a Missionary of Charity.

The parish of St. Teresa of Avila, in Lower Circular Road, Molaali, is where Mother Teresa started her first open clinic. The "house" was the first convent she established in the top floor of the Mike and Agnes Gomes home, on Creek Lane precisely on the territory of St. Teresa's Parish, Calcutta.

Covenant of Consecration to Mary—
to Satiate the Thirst of Jesus

Mary, Mother of Jesus and my mother, moved by a burning desire to live in the closest union with you possible in this life, so as to more surely and fully come to union with your Son, and with you to discover the mystery of his thirst, I resolve to keep this covenant of consecration with you as faithfully and as generously as I am able to with your help.

Since Jesus from the cross gave you to me, I take you as my own. And since Jesus gave me to you, take me as your own. I entrust myself and all I do entirely to you, that you may share your life and heart with me. I give you complete power over me and all that belongs to me, both material and spiritual, that as a mother you may nourish Jesus' thirst within me.

Mary, I depend on you totally as a child on its mother, that in return you may possess me, protect me, and transform me into Jesus. May the light of your faith dispel the darkness of my mind; may your profound humility take the place of my pride; may your contemplation replace the distractions of my wandering imagination; and may your virtues take the place of my sins. Lead me deeper into the mystery of the cross that you may share your experience of Jesus' thirst with me.

O most pure heart of Mary, allow me to enter your heart, to share your interior life. You see and know my needs, help me to do "whatever Jesus tells me" ... that my human needs may be changed into thirst for God alone. I desire to discover, satiate, and proclaim Jesus' thirst, but I know all too well my weakness, nothingness, and sin. Mother, may this covenant of consecration with you be the hidden strength in my life that you may use me to satiate your Son to the full. Let this be my only joy … and you will be the cause of that joy.

Sweet Lord, thy thirst for souls I satiate with my burning love, all for thee. My chalice will be filled with love, sacrifices made all for thee. Evermore, I will quench thy thirst, Lord. Evermore, I will quench thy thirst, Lord, for souls; in union with Mary, our Queen, I will quench thy thirst.

JANUARY 31

Mother Teresa visited Rome many times, and each time it was possible, she would visit the pope, who showed her particular reverence and affection. Mother would then talk with him about her projects, asking for guidance and approval. One of her projects, at the example of her patron saint, Thérèse of Lisieux, was the spiritual adoption of every Catholic priest by a convent of contemplative nuns. Mother Teresa believed that this would foster in the convents a deeper motivation for prayer and sacrifice for priests.

Pope John Paul II listened attentively and said with a smile, "I am a priest, too, Mother, will you have someone adopt me?" Very quick in her response, said and done, Mother Teresa turned to Sr. Nirmala, M.C., (the one taking her place now), and asked her to adopt the pope!

FEBRUARY 1

There is a good theologian, one of the best in India just now. I know him very well and I said to him, "Father, you are talking all day about God. How close you must be to him!" And you know what he said to me? He said, "I may be talking much about God but I may be talking very little to God." It is in the silence of the heart that God speaks.

FEBRUARY 2

We are at his disposal. If he wants us to be sick in bed, if he wants us to proclaim his word in the street, if he wants us to clean the toilets all day, that's all right, everything is all right. We must say, "I belong to you. You can do whatever you like." This is our strength and this is the joy of the Lord.

FEBRUARY 3

When our poor are going through such hard times in regard to food, light, and water, do we give up food that is not absolutely necessary to our health and nutrition? Do we try not to eat outside of regular meals except in times of sickness? Do we take care to use water and light carefully, turning off the taps and putting out any unnecessary lights?

O Jesus, give us great love for the vow of poverty and grace to understand and observe it faithfully.

FEBRUARY 4

What is the Good News? The Good News is that God still loves the world through each one of you. You are God's good news, you are God's love in action. Jesus cannot walk in the streets of Calcutta and in the streets of the world now, so what he does—through me, through you—he walks and touches the poor. Today, God loves the world so much by sending us.

FEBRUARY 5

We do it for Jesus. Do everything for Jesus; this is the way to follow him as our one necessity. Listen to his words and be occupied with his work.

FEBRUARY 6

Jesus will use you to accomplish great things on the condition that you believe much more in his love than in your weakness. Only then, his hand will be free with you.

FEBRUARY 7

We shall not waste our time in looking for extraordinary experiences in our life of prayer but live by pure faith, ever watchful and ready for his coming by doing our day-to-day ordinary duties with extraordinary love and devotion.

FEBRUARY 8

Joy is one of the best safeguards against temptation. The devil is a carrier of dust and dirt and he uses every opportunity to throw what he has at us. But a joyful heart protects us from this dirt. That is because Jesus is there in our joy. Jesus takes full possession of our soul when we surrender to him joyfully.

St. Francis de Sales said, "A sad saint is a bad saint." St. Teresa of Avila worried about her sisters only when she saw them lose their joy. Joy is a source of power for us.

FEBRUARY 9

Let us make our homes real places of love so that we can overcome any hatreds. Love begins at home—everything depends on how we love one another at home. Do not be afraid to love until it hurts because this is how Jesus loved.

Our homes will be what we make them, fervent or tepid, fruitful branches or dry branches. Help one another live in God's love and you will spread the fragrance of his love everywhere.

The Chinese have a very good proverb: The bird of sorrow has to fly, but see that it does not nest in your mind. Yes, suffering is unavoidable, so let us suffer cheerfully. The ups and downs of life must come your way, but you must not let yourself be affected by them in your search for sanctity. Don't be surprised at your failure. You must connect every bit of your life with Holy Communion; all of your failures, your weaknesses, your pride, and your misery. See that, in spite of being tempted, you are not conquered.

A gentleman of the Protestant faith, the son-in-law of Malcolm Muggeridge, told me: "I love you, your work, everything I see, but there is one thing I do not understand: Our Lady. You are full of Mary." I replied to him: "No Mary, no Jesus—no mother, no son."

A few months later he sent me a card with these words printed in big letters: "I believe, no Mary, no Jesus! This has changed my life."

FEBRUARY 12

Total surrender to God means to be entirely at the disposal of the Father just as Jesus and Mary were. This is not asking anything extraordinary: We give ourselves completely to him because he has given himself completely to us. God does not need to explain himself to us when we put ourselves entirely at his disposal.

We must ask ourselves: How have we given ourselves to God? How have we allowed God into our lives? What is our surrender to him?

FEBRUARY 13

How do we become humble? By accepting humiliations. Whenever you are scolded, mistreated, or called names, grab such an occasion with both hands. That humiliation will make you holy. Accept it.

Loving trust in God implies trust in his almightiness, his infinite wisdom, and his unfailing love. He loves me. I'm not here just to fill a place, just to be a number. He has made me for a purpose. He will fulfill it if I don't put any obstacle in his way.

We must cultivate that sacred silence which makes people remember the words of Jesus: See how they love one another. How often we find ourselves speaking of the faults of another. How often our conversation is about someone who is not present. Yet see the compassion of Christ toward Judas, the man who received so much love yet betrayed his own master. But the master kept the sacred silence and did not betray Judas. Jesus could have easily spoken in public—as we often do—telling the hidden intentions and deeds of Judas to others. But he didn't. Instead, he showed mercy and charity. Rather than condemning Judas, he called him his friend.

FEBRUARY 16

Confession makes the soul strong because a really good confession—the confession of a child in sin coming back to the Father—always begets humility, and humility is strength. We may go to confession as often as we want and to whom we want, but we are not encouraged to seek spiritual direction from any and every source. The confessional is not a place for useless conversation or gossip. The topic should be our sins, our sorrow, our forgiveness: how to overcome our temptations, how to practice virtue, how to increase in the love of God.

FEBRUARY 17

We must improve our prayer and, flowing from that, our charity toward others. It can be difficult to pray when we don't know how, but we can help ourselves through the use of silence. Souls of prayer are souls of great silence. This silence takes a lot of sacrifice, but if we really want to pray, we must be ready to take that step now. Without this first step toward silence, we will not be able to reach our goal, which is union with God.

Learn to be humble by doing all the humble work and doing it for Jesus. You cannot learn humility from books; you learn it by accepting humiliations. Humiliations are not meant to torture us; they are gifts from God. These little humiliations—if we accept them with joy—will help us to be holy, to have a meek and humble heart like Jesus.

If we have a pure heart, then we can see God. If we cannot see God then we must ask: Is there something between us and our Lord? Sometimes there is a darkness that brings us closer to God, troubles and trials through which we must persevere. But sometimes there is a darkness that is dividing our love for God. With chastity, though, there is no dividing, no separation, there is only a cleaving to God. This cleaving means we are woven together with God like the threads of a cloth that cannot be separated. The only reason for our existence is to live in him, for him, by him, and with him.

FEBRUARY 20

Holiness is union with God. When we are holy—in prayer and action alike—we come from God in Christ and go to God through Christ.

Jesus said, "Love one another as I have loved you." These words should be a light to us, a flame consuming the selfishness that prevents the growth of holiness.

FEBRUARY 21

When I hear all the pain and suffering caused by idle remarks and unkindness, I think of our Lord, who told the people they should throw a stone at the sinful woman only if they were without sin. All the people went away because they knew that Jesus knew their sins. When we are tempted to speak uncharitably or to bring up someone's past failures, let us hear Jesus say: Throw the stone only if you are free from sin.

Resist anything that leads to moodiness. Our prayer each day should be, "Let the joy of the Lord be my strength." Cheerfulness and joy were Our Lady's strength. This made her a willing handmaid of God. Only joy could have given her the strength to go in haste over the hills of Judea to her cousin Elizabeth, there to do the work of a handmaid. If we are to be true handmaids of the Lord, then we too, each day, must go cheerfully in haste over the hills of difficulties.

FEBRUARY 23

We read in the gospel that Jesus said, "I have come to do the will of my Father." We can apply this to ourselves for we have come to do the will of God. Jesus said, again and again, "Thy will be done," and we say the same thing through our obedience to him.

Obedience is something spiritual since it is found also in heaven. Disobedience was the first sin. Lucifer refused to submit, refused to obey. This was true, too, for our first parents, Adam and Eve, who refused to obey and ate what was forbidden by God. When we disobey, it is a continuation of that first sin.

February 24

We have dedicated ourselves to give wholehearted free service to the poor. Do they rejoice in our service? When they see us, do their hearts leap for joy as St. John's did in his mother's womb when Mary brought Jesus into his house? Do we really go to the poor filled with Jesus, as Mary was, always ready to give only Jesus to the poor? Is our service to the poor devoted and tender? Do we serve them as Mary served Elizabeth?

February 25

A Missionary of Charity is a person who joins the Bread of Life and the hungry Christ, prayer and wholehearted free service. If you cannot pray, you cannot stay.

FEBRUARY 26

You must forgive and forget all the difficult things of yesterday for yesterday has gone. Tomorrow has not yet come. But you have today to love Jesus as he loves you, with a deep personal love. Do not be afraid. God will give you all the graces you need if you allow him to make you holy through prayer and sacrifices, penance and hard work.

FEBRUARY 27

Chastity is not only our ability to give, but more, our ability to accept God's gift. Is it your desire to follow Christ perfectly? Are you resolved to live in chastity? Chastity is a sign of the kingdom of heaven.

FEBRUARY 28

A rich man came to Shishu Bhavan (the house of un-wanted babies) and said he would give whatever the sisters would ask. He wanted to give a generator. This costs thousands. I told him "no." Today a generator, tomorrow a washing machine. He said, "Mother, all these years I have been producing all kinds of things to make more and more money, but from the time I came into contact with the poor, I want to give." So he gave us some kerosene lamps. We must be convinced of the freedom of our poverty and keep to the most humble means.

FEBRUARY 29

We forget that in the silence of the heart God speaks, and from the fullness of the heart we speak. Only when we have heard him in the silence of our hearts, only when we have learned to listen to God in the silence of our hearts, only then can we say: I pray. There is no either/or about prayer and love. We can't say we have either prayer or love: There is no prayer without love and no love without prayer.

MARCH 1

During Lent, free your mind from all that is not Jesus. This will improve your spirit of prayer and recollection. If you find it difficult to pray, then say again and again: "Jesus, come into my heart. Pray in me and with me that I may learn from you how to pray."

Praying the rosary as you walk or travel is a beautiful means to constant prayer.

MARCH 2

Be extra careful to do penance, especially during the holy time of Lent. Make it a point to be faithful in small details. Jesus said that penance is necessary if we want to conquer the world, the flesh, and the devil.

MARCH 3

Our thoughts often turn to the passion and death of our Lord, and we long to share his pain with him. What is the pain of Jesus? It is the pain of loving and not being loved in return. He has loved us with an everlasting love, and what do we give him in return? We allow our minds to be preoccupied with little things and so spend many hours without thinking of Jesus. And yet our hearts and minds, bodies and soul, belong only to him.

Let us meditate on the sufferings of Christ each day. We often pray, "Jesus, let me share in your pain." Yet when a thorn of thoughtlessness comes our way or a little spittle in the form of an uncharitable remark, we forget that this is the time to share with him his shame and his pain.

March 4

Jesus spent forty days in prayer before beginning his public life. He often retired alone and spent the night in silence and prayer.

The fruit of silence is prayer.

The fruit of prayer is faith.

The fruit of faith is love.

The fruit of love is service.

The fruit of service is peace.

Let us provide each other an atmosphere of peace and quiet which will facilitate prayer, work, study, and rest.

March 5

Humility is nothing but truth. What have we got that we have not received, asks St. Paul. If I have received everything, what good have I of my own? If we are convinced of this, we will never raise our head in pride.

If we are humble, nothing will touch us, neither praise nor disgrace. If we are blamed, we will not be discouraged if we are praised, we will not be driven away.

Take time to think about the Eucharist. God himself became so small that just two fingers can hold him in the host. A small child or a dying person can receive him. The Eucharist is beyond understanding, to be accepted only in deep faith and love.

Jesus deliberately left us the Eucharist to help us remember all that he came to do. In the Gospels, there are only a few words describing his passion and death. These few words—which we could so easily forget—tell us that he was crowned with thorns, scourged, and spat upon. The Gospels avoid lengthy explanations in their description of the passion, telling us that he was scourged but not how many times or even what the whip was made of.

But Jesus understands our human nature. He understands that when something is far from the eyes it can be far from the heart as well. Just imagine what life would be like without the Eucharist. What would there be to make us love him? What would there be to make us give up everything? I don't think any of us would be here without the Eucharist.

MARCH 7

God is the friend of silence. His language is silence. "Be still and know that I am God." He requires us to be silent to discover him. Jesus spent forty days in silence before beginning his public life. He often retired alone, spent the night on the mountain in silence and prayer. He who spoke with authority spent his early life in silence. We need to be alone with God in silence to be renewed and to be transformed. Silence gives us a new outlook on life. In it we are filled with the energy of God himself that makes us do all things with joy.

MARCH 8

Each one of us should enter into the passion of Christ with greater love. He looks for one to console him, to comfort him. Do you try enough to be that one? Today, Christ suffers in many ways in the despised: hungry for love, he looks to you; thirsty for kindness, he begs from you; longing for loyalty, he hopes in you. Sick and in prison, he looks for your friendship. Homeless, he asks for shelter in your heart.

Will you be that one to him?

St. Paul said, "I can do all things in him who strengthens me." You must come to the conviction that with Jesus, you can do all things. Even the weakness that troubles you, you can get rid of with him.

Sometimes, in the church, there is a struggle when we see one another's weakness. Unless we have trust, it is impossible to live a pure and holy life. We must have respect for each other. We must realize that if God chose me, he chose you, too. If he trusts me, he trusts you, too. We should find out what is nice in the other person and bow to Jesus in the heart of that person. Deepen your love for one another.

Learn from Our Lady to have the same trust that she placed in St. Joseph. Learn from Our Lady, who, when she saw Jesus humiliated and scourged, was not afraid to claim him as her son. Let us pray to her to fill our hearts with that trust so that nothing and nobody will separate us from the love of Christ.

Jesus loved us to the end, to the very limit, dying on the cross. We must have this same love which comes from within, from our union with Christ. Such love must be as normal to us as living and breathing. St. Thérèse of Lisieux said: "When I act and think with charity, I feel it is Jesus who works within me. The closer I am united with him, the more I love all the other dwellers in Carmel."

Our works of charity are nothing but the overflow of our love for God. Therefore, the one who is most united to God loves others the most. To understand and practice this, we need to pray, for prayer unites us with God and overflows upon others.

MARCH 11

We are commanded to love God and our neighbor equally, without difference. We don't have to look for the opportunities to fill this command, they're all around us, twenty-four hours a day. You must open your eyes wide so that you can see the opportunities to give wholehearted, free service right where you are, in your family. If you don't give such service in your family, you will not be able to give it to those outside your home.

MARCH 12

Be kind and loving with each other, for you cannot love Christ in his distressing disguise if you cannot love Jesus in the heart of your neighbors. Love, to be truly love, must be fed on sacrifice. Be generous in accepting all the sacrifices that come every day on your way. Then you will be able to say in all sincerity, "My God and my all."

MARCH 13

Prayer is nothing but that oneness with Christ. As Scripture says in St. Paul, "I live no longer, but Christ lives in me." Christ prays in me, Christ thinks in me, Christ looks through my eyes, Christ speaks through my words, Christ works with my hands, Christ walks with my feet, Christ loves with my heart.

MARCH 14

To surrender to God means that we offer him our will, our reason, our life. We do this in pure faith, even if our soul is in darkness. Truly, trials and sufferings are the surest test of blind surrender.

Surrender is also a sign of our true love for God and for souls. If we really love others, we must be ready to take their place, to take their sins upon ourselves and to expiate them through penance and continual mortification. We must be living holocausts for those souls who are most in need.

MARCH 15

On the cross they tried to give Jesus a bitter drink, like a drug, but he did not use it because his thirst was for love, for souls, for you and me.

MARCH 16

Be faithful to the time spent in prayer and make sure that at least half of your prayer is spent in silence. This will bring you closer to Jesus. If you deepen your prayer life you will grow in holiness and obtain many graces for the souls entrusted to your care. Deepen your love for one another by praying for each other and by sharing thoughts and graces you have received in prayer and reading.

MARCH 17

When someone is doing something to hurt you, don't turn inward, turn toward that person. He is hurting himself. You must learn to forgive, knowing that we all need forgiveness. If you want to be true to God, you must learn from Jesus to be meek, humble, and pure.

MARCH 18

We trust in the power of the name of Jesus and also in the intercessory power of St. Joseph. When we first started our society, there were times when we had nothing. We kept a picture of St. Joseph which we turned face down during those times we were in great need. This reminded us to ask for his intercession. When something came in, we turned it right side up.

One day, a priest wanted to print some holy cards to

help stimulate an increase of devotion to St. Joseph. He came to me for money, but I had only one rupee in the house. I debated whether or not to give it to him but I did. That evening, he came back and gave me an envelope full of money—one hundred rupees. Someone had stopped him and given him the money for Mother Teresa.

MARCH 19

St. Joseph knew, when Mary became pregnant, that this child was not his child. He saw that she was pregnant but he didn't know how. If he had gone to the high priest, she would have been stoned to death. Do you see the charity and thoughtfulness of St. Joseph? If we have that same kind of charity and thoughtfulness toward each other, our families will become the abode of the Most High. How beautiful our families will become where there is total thoughtfulness for others.

MARCH 20

As St. Paul said, "It is not I that live but Christ that lives within me." Our life of consecrated chastity should make us say the same thing. Just as in marriage there is no divorce, so there is no divorce for us from God. What God has put together, no one can separate, both in the married and in the religious life.

March 21

We have to love until it hurts. It is not enough to say, "I love." We must put that love into a living action. And how do we do that? By giving until it hurts.

March 22

It is not enough to say yes to God when he has called us for himself. It's very important to put that yes into a living action. And how do we put that into a living action? By our total surrender to him. We understand that he has chosen us for himself—all that follows is that we allow him to use us without consulting us.

We are human beings and we like to know exactly what he wants, how he wants, and so on. But if we really want to be only all for Jesus, it is important that we give him a free hand to do with us what he wants, as he wants. Only then can we really say we are only all for Jesus.

We must be present with and to the Lord and with and to our community, our family, in silence as Mary practiced silence. We begin with silence of the will, that is, willing nothing but the will of God. Begin here and the rest will come. The Holy Spirit will come upon you and you will experience silence. Guard and protect it with love and you will become a garden enclosed. Silence is the soil for the seed of the Word.

MARCH 24

The most wonderful part of redemption began in such a humble way. God did not send Gabriel to the palace of the great and rich but to the young girl Mary in the one-room cottage at Nazareth. She asked but one question of the angel who announced she would be the mother of the Savior: How could this be? And when he explained, she, being full of grace, offered herself as the handmaid of the Lord.

This was why she was chosen, because although she was full of grace, she was also full of humility. She didn't think of the grace of the Son of God within her. She didn't dwell on the joy and sorrow that were hers as the Mother of God and of mankind. She only thought of how to serve, of how to fulfill her vocation as the handmaid of the Lord.

March 25

The Annunciation was Our Lady's first communion day. Mary entrusted the angel with a deep loving trust because he brought the Good News, he was God's messenger. This is our spirit too.

Just think of almighty God in the womb of Mary, locked in. He had to cling helplessly to his mother. This was the total surrender of Christ. Again, nailed to the cross, he could not move. Again today, he is bound in the tabernacle. This is total surrender.

March 26

"Hail Mary, full of grace, the Lord is with you." When Mary heard this greeting of the angel, she was troubled and wondered what it might mean. Even Mary, sinless and perfect, was troubled and wondered. She was not a statue without human feelings but was like you and me in many ways.

And then the angel said to her, "Do not be afraid, for nothing is impossible with God. You shall bear a son and name him Jesus." And Mary said, "Behold the handmaid of the Lord, be it done unto me according to your word."

All the evil in the world came through that first act of disobedience, the eating of that one apple. It is the same for us. One act of deliberate disobedience will bring lots of evil into our life.

Understand that God is calling you through obedience, even if he does not call you directly. In the Annunciation, God did not speak to Our Lady directly but through an angel. By doing what the angel said, Mary obeyed God. It is the same for us. God does not speak to us directly but through our superiors. They are instruments in his hands.

How often we say, "I wish I hadn't seen that thing," yet we do little to overcome the desire to see everything.

We must have silence in our mind and heart as well. Our Lady kept all things in her heart and practiced silence that brought her close to God. She never had to regret anything. Observe what Mary did when Joseph was troubled by her pregnancy. One word from her would have cleared his mind but she didn't say that word. Our Lord himself worked a miracle to clear her name. He would do that for us, too, if we would be convinced of the necessity of silence.

MARCH 29

Mary had a call and a mission, and she went through a process of discernment to accept them. She responded to the angel in obedience and rejoiced, saying "yes." All mankind rejoices with her in her "yes." She had been chosen as the Queen of Heaven and Earth, yet she did not go in search of glory or even to tell Joseph. The first thing she did as the Mother of God was to go in haste to serve her cousin Elizabeth.

MARCH 30

See how Our Lady obeyed the angel, responding, "Be it done unto me according to your word." Whose word? The angel's, who took the place of God, being sent by God to her. She, the Queen of Heaven, obeyed an angel. See how she obeyed St. Joseph, with love and submission, without any excuse.

In 1978, Mother needed an audience with the pope to receive the first gathering of Italian co-workers. Arriving in Rome, she asked me to come along to help her on her way to the Vatican. As we reached the pope's private apartment, we were taken to a waiting room by his secretary, Monsignor Macchi, and as we were waiting, she turned to me and said, "Brother, what did we come here for?" She was completely oblivious as to the primary reasons we were there. As I reminded her, she quickly recomposed herself in the recitation of the rosary. As soon as we left the Apostolic Palace, with the sun already shining brightly on Rome, I turned to Mother, surprised at her forgetfulness of the moment before. I asked, "Mother, what in the world made you so distracted that you forgot the reason we had come to the Vatican?"

Her reply was with a twinkle of holy mischief in her eyes. "All those empty rooms we had to cross before coming to the pope's apartment, I was counting in my head how many beds I could put for our people!"

Only a few years passed before Pope John Paul II built a seventy-bed facility on the Vatican grounds for the homeless and destitute of Rome. He called it *Dono di Maria* (Gift of Mary), since that year (1987) in Rome was a special year dedicated to Mary, "The Marian Year."

APRIL 1

Come, O blessed Spirit of knowledge and light, and grant that I may perceive the will of the Father. Show me the nothingness of earthly things, that I may realize their vanity and use them only for your glory and my own salvation, looking ever beyond them to you and your eternal reward.

APRIL 2

When we meditate on the passion of our Lord, we should examine our conscience to see what sin of ours caused that special pain to Jesus. We can make reparation and share that pain by doubling our penance.

We should keep strict custody of the eyes. We should hold clean thoughts in our minds. We should keep greater silence of the heart. In that silence we will hear his words of comfort and, in turn, be able to comfort Jesus in the distressing disguise of the poor.

Jesus said that penance is necessary if we want to conquer the world, the flesh, and the devil. Sacrifice, if it is to be real, must cost us, must hurt, must empty us of self. Let us think about the passion of Christ, his sufferings. The point of such meditation is not just to have our feelings roused. Rather, our meditation should lead us to change as we cooperate with God's grace in real sacrifices of self.

Let us preach the peace of Christ as he did, by going about doing good. He didn't stop his works of charity even though people hated him and tried to spoil his Father's work. He just went about doing good. Cardinal Newman wrote: "Help me to spread your fragrance everywhere I go. Let me preach you without preaching, not by words but by example."

April 5

May the risen Christ be your joy and peace. May the joy of the risen Christ be your strength in your work, your way to the Father, your light to guide you, your Bread of Life. Remember that the passion of Christ always ends in the joy of the resurrection. When you feel in your own heart the suffering Christ, remember that the resurrection has to come. The joy of Easter will dawn.

April 6

Deepen your prayer life and you will grow in holiness and obtain many graces for the souls entrusted to your care.

Remember, a pure heart will see God. You must have the conviction, each day, that you belong to Jesus crucified, that nothing will separate you from his love. This conviction is the sure way to great holiness, and if you are holy, you will be able to pray effectively for the work. The fruit of holiness is what makes us contemplatives at the heart of the world.

Jesus wants us to love each other as the Father has loved him. There is no greater love than the love for one another in our families, but there is so much hurt instead of love, so much bitterness instead of sweetness, so much noise instead of silence.

If there is no love in our home, first let us examine our prayer life. Is it faithful, is it true, is it constant, is it full, is it so real that in the silence of our hearts we can hear him speak? If we only knew the art, the joy, the fruitfulness of silence, our homes would become the sunshine of God's love, the burning flame of God's love in action.

APRIL 8

May the joy and the love of the risen Jesus be always with you, in you, and among you so that you become the true witnesses of the Father's love for the world. Remember: "God so loved the world that he gave his only begotten Son." Let us also love God so much that we give ourselves to him in each other and in the poor.

We can do this only by fidelity to Christ, by belonging to him alone, and by tender and thoughtful love for each other. How beautiful it is to see this love for each other be a living reality. Young sisters, have this deep love and respect for your elder sisters. Older sisters, treat your younger sisters with respect and love for they, like you, belong to Jesus.

He has chosen each one of you for himself, to be his light and his love in the world. The simplest way to become his light is to be kind and loving, thoughtful and sincere with each other. As Jesus said: "By this they will know that you are my disciples."

APRIL 9

All over the world, there is terrible suffering, terrible hunger for love. So bring prayer into your family, bring it to your children. Teach them to pray, for a child who prays is a happy child. A family that prays is a united family. We hear of so many broken families. Why are they broken? I think because they never pray together. They are never one in prayer before the Lord.

Dear Priest, Co-Worker of Christ,

You have said "yes" to Jesus and he has taken you at your word. The Word of God became Jesus, the poor one. And so, this terrible emptiness you experience....

God cannot fill what is full, he can only fill emptiness, deep poverty, and your "yes" is the beginning of being or becoming empty. It is not how much we really have to give but how empty we are, so that we can receive him fully in our life. Let him live his life in you today.

APRIL 11

The joy of the risen Lord is the sunshine of our Father's love. The joy of Jesus is the hope of eternal happiness. The joy of Jesus is the flame of burning love. Easter is this joy. However, you cannot have joy without sacrifice. That is why Good Friday comes before Easter.

APRIL 12

Let us beg Our Lady to make our hearts as meek and humble as her Son's. From her and within her the heart of Jesus was formed. We can learn much from Our Lady, who was so humble because she was all for God.

APRIL 13

Charity for the poor is like a living flame: the more dry the wood, the brighter it burns.

APRIL 14

Our lives are founded on Jesus and Mary and so we ask ourselves: What was their total surrender? Scripture tells us that Jesus, though he was God, "did not count equality with God something to be grasped at. Rather, he emptied himself and took the form of a slave, being born in the likeness of men." This was complete surrender, but it can be difficult to understand Jesus because he is God. Mary, however, is completely one of us. She loved, she surrendered, she emptied herself.

APRIL 15

Serve God joyfully. Let there be no sadness in your life: the only true sorrow is sin.

Jesus said, "If a man loves me he will keep my commandment.... Love one another as I have loved you." He said that if we love him, his Father would love us and come to us and make his home with us.

Through our works of love, we bring about an increase of grace and a growth in divine love. Jesus will manifest himself through us to each other and to the world, and by his love, others will know that we are his disciples. In spite of all our defects, God is in love with us and keeps using us to light the light of love and compassion in the world. So give Jesus a big smile and a hearty thank you.

When are we truly humble?

When we refuse to judge and criticize others.

When we foster kindly thoughts toward others.

When we rejoice in the good others accomplish for Jesus.

When we find an excuse for the failures of others.

When we are happy and cheerful with the poor, the sick, and the dying.

When we have joy in the hour of humiliation.

Then we are truly humble after the heart of Jesus.

April 18

Sometime back, a high government official said, "You are doing social work and we also are doing the same. But we are doing it for something and you are doing it for somebody." To do our work, we have to be in love with God.

April 19

Christ obeyed because he loved his Father. He was equal to the Father but did not feel it was below his dignity to obey. He went to Nazareth with Mary and Joseph and was obedient to them. It was enough for Jesus that the Father had given authority to the high priest, to Herod, and to Pilate.

Much of the suffering inside and outside the church today is caused solely by a misunderstanding of freedom and renewal. We cannot be free unless we are able to surrender our will freely to the will of God. We must obey with full freedom in a spirit of unity and submission and through wholehearted free service to Christ in his distressing disguise.

Obedience means total surrender and wholehearted free service to the poorest of the poor. All the difficulties that come in our work are the result of disobedience. The obedience of the Little Flower, St. Thérèse of Lisieux, was beautiful and complete. She obeyed her superior even in things that might seem stupid—but for God, nothing is stupid. The smaller the thing, the greater the love.

Moodiness is nothing else but the fruit of pride.

Jesus said: "Whatever you do to the least of my brethren you do it to me." If in my name you give a glass of water, you gave it to me. If in my name you receive a little child, you received me. I was hungry, I was naked, I was homeless, you did it to me. So this is what Jesus came to teach us: how to love one another. Not big things, small things, but great love.

APRIL 23

A clean heart is a free heart. A free heart can love Christ with an undivided love in chastity, convinced that nothing and nobody will separate it from his love. Purity, chastity, and virginity created a special beauty in Mary that attracted God's attention. He showed his great love for the world by giving Jesus to her.

APRIL 24

As you grow, you have still to learn. I'm still learning though I am fifty-three years in the convent. I am learning from you. We have to learn from each other. Jesus took a little child and put him in front of the apostles. Love begins here. That little kindness, care, compassion, that is the hidden treasure, the growth in holiness. We know where it is, let us go for it!

Let us make our Society a faithful, living branch on the vine, which is Jesus. With great determination and humility, we must love and serve each other. Then together, we will make something beautiful for God. If we are of one heart, full of love, if we love each other and the poor we serve, then we will grow together in holiness. Holiness is the main reason for the existence of the Missionaries of Charity—and achieving holiness should not be difficult because in giving wholehearted free service to the poorest of the poor, we are with Jesus twenty-four hours a day.

Poverty makes us free. We need to experience the joy of poverty. We choose poverty, we choose not to have things, unlike the poorest of the poor who are forced to be poor. If we do not have something, it is because we choose not to have it. In this, we are free because nothing belongs to us. Our poverty means that we do not have the kind of shoes we may want or the house we may want. We cannot keep things or give anything away or lend anything of value. We have nothing. We own nothing. This is the experience of poverty.

APRIL 27

Jesus prayed that "all may be one as you, Father, are in me and I in you." All the members of the Society form one family and all have the same obligations, the same privileges, and work for the same purpose.

Just as Jesus prayed for his disciples, so St. Paul urges the first Christians in the same way. "May God, the source of all patience and encouragement, enable you to live in perfect harmony with one another." Be of one mind and have peace and the God of peace and love will be with you.

APRIL 28

If we keep silence, we will not be uncharitable. Let us ask Our Lady to teach us that silence which will help us to pray and listen and love as she loves. Silence is one of those things that will help us to live only for Jesus.

If we really understand silence, we understand prayer.

We are commanded to love God and our neighbor equally, on the same level. There is no difference. Love for our neighbor must be equal to our love for God. We don't have to search for opportunities, we have them twenty-four hours a day with those around us. How is it that we do not see and we miss these opportunities?

Help me to spread thy fragrance: thy fragrance is joy!

How many big sinners have changed their lives through our work only because of the touch of joy?

A Ramakrisha Mission leader came to Burdwan [West Bengal] where I had been asked to go since they had raised some money for leprosy patients. After I spoke to the assembly thanking them for the donation, the Ramakrisha leader stood up and said, "When I look at the sisters of Mother Teresa walking in the streets, praying so joyfully, I believe that Jesus Christ has come once again walking the path of the world doing good."

A great silence fell on the audience, interrupted only by someone saying, "Has he become a Christian?"

We must examine ourselves by asking: are we really Jesus' image to the people of Calcutta? to the world?

MAY 1

People all over the world offer Mary, our mother, beautiful gifts and cover her altar with flowers. We have no material gifts to offer her but let us give her flowers of kindness, the flower of a welcoming smile. On this beautiful feast day, let us crown her with the fragrant flowers of love, gentleness, meekness, and humility toward one another.

MAY 2

Mary thought only of how to serve, of how to fulfill her vocation as handmaid of the Lord.

The life of Mary is so much like ours. When God first called us, he had prepared us through our parents and friends, just as he had prepared Mary. He sent his messenger to the poor—to Mary—to tell of his choice just as he tells us of his choice of us. Our first question was also like Mary's: How can this be? How can we become Missionaries of Charity? Then we, with Our Lady, declared before heaven and earth: Behold, the handmaid of the Lord, behold, I come to do God's will.

Prayer helps us to love each other because when Jesus is with us there are no distractions. Failure and loss of grace come from the neglect of prayer because prayer is the food of the spiritual life. We starve the spirit when we neglect prayer, and loss of grace is unavoidable. Let us ask Mary to teach us how to pray as she taught Jesus during all those years he was with her in Nazareth.

Mary showed complete trust in God by agreeing to be used as an instrument in his plan of salvation. She trusted him in spite of her nothingness because she knew he who is mighty could do great things in her and through her. Once she said "yes" to him, she never doubted. She was just a young woman, but she belonged to God and nothing nor anyone could separate her from him.

May 5

We must pray, understand, love, and live the freedom of true poverty. God forbid that our people reject us because of our riches.

May 6

Holiness is not a luxury reserved for a few but a simple duty for each of us. Holiness is a great thing, but it becomes very simple when we belong fully to Our Lady. If we turn constantly to Our Lady, she will teach us how to grow in holiness through obedience. Our sanctification is her main duty. When we really belong to Mary, we will find obedience to be the greatest means for growing in holiness and living in the constant presence of God.

May 7

A zeal for souls is both the result and the proof of a true love for God. We cannot but be consumed with the desire for saving souls. This is the greatest and the dearest interest of Jesus. Zeal is the test of love, and the test of zeal is complete devotion to his cause. We must spend our life and our energy in the work for souls.

MAY 8

When, at the very beginning after leaving my convent at Loreto Entally, I arrived in Creek Lane, Calcutta, alone, I had only a box and five rupees. A man from Air India wanted to give me a nice suitcase to carry the few things I had with me. I said to him, "There is no shame in carrying a cardboard box." So also, there is no shame in asking when we need guidance or help. Is it not better for me to ask, than from pride and ignorance to do what is wrong?

MAY 9

Every day at Communion, I tell Jesus: If you know the M.C. Society is going to lose the gift, let it die before my eyes.

May 10

Scripture tells us that Mary pondered Jesus' words in her heart. When we have received the Living Bread and are communicating with Christ in our heart, we should remember what Our Lady must have felt when the Holy Spirit overpowered her and she was full of grace—filled with the body of Christ, her child, within her. The Spirit within her was so strong that immediately she rose and went in haste to serve her cousin Elizabeth.

Each Holy Communion, each breaking of the Bread of Life, should produce a similar response in us. The same Jesus who came to Mary and was made flesh comes to us and becomes our life. Like her, we should be in haste to give this life of Jesus to others.

May 11

Let us beg Our Lady to make our hearts as meek and humble as her Son's was. It is from her and in her that the heart of Jesus was formed.

How much we can learn from Mary! She was humble because she was all for God. She was full of grace and so the Almighty could use her. We need to say to Our Lady: "Tell Jesus that we have no wine"—the wine of meekness, humility, of kindness and sweetness. She is sure to say to us, "Do whatever he tells you."

Older sisters, you must be the shining light of Christ to the younger sisters. Let them see your total surrender to God. Demonstrate that surrender by accepting whatever he gives you and giving whatever he takes from you. Your prompt, blind, simple, and cheerful obedience will teach them what loving trust means. Your joyful smile will show them how grateful you are to God for having chosen you to serve him in his poor. Let us not forget that the aim of our Society is to quench the thirst of Jesus for souls.

Knowledge of Christ in his poor will lead us to personal love. This love can only become our light and joy in cheerful service of each other. Don't forget, we need each other. Our lives would be empty without each other. How can we love God and his poor if we do not love each other, with whom we live and break the Bread of Life daily?

MAY 14

It will console our Lord and make our mother Mary very happy if we try to understand the importance of obedience. Obedience to the will of God begets in our soul unfailing peace, inward joy, and close union with him. Let us renew our commitment to this obedience at the cross of Jesus, thinking especially of the wound in his right foot. Have you noticed that usually, when we walk, we put our right foot first? So let us renew our commitment there, at the wound in his foot, acknowledging that we will not take even one step except in obedience.

MAY 15

Let us ask the Lord to grant us one very special grace—to love Our Lady, especially through all the work we do for Jesus, with Jesus, and to Jesus. We must ask him to deepen our love for Mary, making it more personal and intimate. We want to:

Love her as he loved her.

Be a cause of joy to her as he was.

Keep close to her as he did.

Share everything with her, even the cross, as he did when she stood near the cross on Calvary.

We must love her unconditionally, trust her fully, abandon ourselves to her totally and without reserve. Nothing is impossible for those who call Mary their mother. During the day, let us often raise our hearts to her and ask her how we can love God as she loved him, that we, too, can love him with her heart.

MAY 16

Our Lady knows us by heart and she will lead us to the surest and quickest path to holiness. Remember that scene in the Gospel at the marriage feast at Cana? Only Mary noticed that the wine was running short. She felt bad for the young couple and wanted to spare them the humiliation of not having enough for their guests. What did she do? Without making any fuss, she quietly approached Jesus and simply said, "They have no wine."

See the charity of Mary! See how she noticed the needs of others and was so delicate in speaking to Jesus.

MAY 17

What if the servant at the wedding feast had not obeyed Jesus' simple request to fill the pots with water and serve the guests? If he had not obeyed, we would not have the joy of knowing Jesus' love for his Mother and the Mother's faith in the power of her Son. She still tells us, "Do whatever he tells you." Obey and you will experience the joy of loving and being loved.

MAY 18

The beginning of holiness is found in faithfulness to prayer. May each of us grow in holiness through prayer.

If we pray—we will believe.

If we believe—we will love.

If we love—we will serve.

Only then will we put our love for God into action, through service to Christ in the distressing disguise of the poor.

MAY 19

When little Sunil, now twenty-one years old, was one and a half years old, his father died. In despair the mother drank something and the little one sat near her until she died. I took him to Shishu Bhavan and he did not want to eat; I suppose he wanted to die like his mother. I told Sr. Agnes, "Try to do something for him." She must have looked like his mother ... because he began to eat and recovered. The other day he came to me and said, "I want to do for the poor children what you have done for me."

Every home should feel the sunshine of God's love radiating through it. Remember that he has called you by name, you are his, you are precious to him, he loves you. Those we live with belong to him, are precious to him. Such knowledge should become the burning flame of God's love in our homes. May we each grow into the likeness of Christ through love for each other.

MAY 21

The Holy Family consisted of Jesus, Mary, and Joseph, not just Jesus alone. For the family to be complete, it was necessary to have Joseph the carpenter alongside the greatness of Jesus and the spotlessness of Mary. So too, in our churches, several people may be very capable but they do not make up the community. We need others to complete the team.

MAY 22

Once, when I was traveling by car in Delhi, I saw a man lying at the side of the road, half on the sidewalk, half on the street. It was a busy road and cars were passing by but no one stopped to see if he was all right. I stopped the car and the sisters and I picked him up. The sisters were surprised that I had seen him since they had not.

If our heart is pure and free from sin then we will see God. Unless we give free and wholehearted service to those we live with, then we will be unable to give it to the poor outside.

MAY 23

We go about doing good to the people and so they surround us with love and respect and trust. This is why we need humility—to protect us in danger, to guard us from falls, to guarantee the fruitfulness of our works of charity.

Our life, being so much in the public eye, has the more need of humility. It is beautiful to see the humility of Christ. Scripture says: "Though he was in the form of God, he did not deem equality with God something to be grasped at, but emptied himself ... being born in the likeness of men."

Our ideal is no one but Jesus.

We have renounced sin, we have renounced the world—but what do we mean by "renounce"? We mean that we "give up." When we join religious life, each of us has to tell our mother and father that we want to go and we want their blessing. This can be difficult because a parent's love is beautiful and precious.

I remember when I told my mother of my vocation, she locked herself in her room. She didn't want me to go. She was a holy person and, locked up in her room, praying, she was able to accept my vocation. Sometimes I think, though, that it is my mother who will judge me, rather than Jesus, because I have given her lots of sorrow.

Recently, I got a letter from a girl who said, "I know I have a vocation but I will let my mother decide." The mother wrote back to say that she was willing, if this is what Jesus wants. This is what vocation means, that Jesus has called us by name.

If your heart is full of worldly things, you cannot hear the voice of God. But when you have listened to his voice in the silence of your heart, then your heart is filled. Then, from the fullness of the heart the mouth will speak.

You may be writing, then the fullness of your heart may come to your hand also. Your heart may speak through writing. Your heart may speak through your eyes also. When you look at people, they must be able to see God in your eyes.

The fullness of the heart is expressed in our eyes, in our touch, in what we write, in what we say, the way we walk, the way we receive, the way we need. That is the fullness of the heart expressing itself in many different ways.

MAY 26

Let us give Mary full liberty to use us for the glory of her Son, for if we really belong to her then our holiness is secure. We can only learn love for Mary on our knees and through the rosary. Let us improve our praying of the rosary, and let us ask Mary to teach us how to pray as she taught Jesus in all the years he was with her in Nazareth. Our Lady is the mother of the church and our mother, a woman of purity, poverty, obedience, and charity. Bring Our Lady fully into your life at home and in the homes of the poor.

MAY 27

Poverty is our dowry. The less we have, the more we can give. The more we have, the less we give. There are no complications and yet we complicate our lives so much, by so many additions.

If I were to give the Nobel Prize to anybody, I would give it to the devil. I think he is the wisest because of the way he works: he is the father of lies. He has infinite patience, he keeps waiting and waiting until you have given in.

Find Jesus and you will find peace.

Mother was invited to bring her sisters to Cuba. She asked me to help her find a little statue of Mary to give General Fidel Castro. She was received very well by the general, who gave her permission to attend to the terminally ill patients of the island; however, he explained to her that there were no poor people in Cuba since the revolution had done away with poverty.

At the moment of departure, Mother gave General Castro the statue of Mary and asked him to pray for her. Castro replied, "Mother, my prayer for you is my service for you."

Later, someone from Cuba sent a little statue of Our Lady of Charity, "La Caridad del Cobre," to Mother Teresa. I was in Calcutta at the time, and Mother called me and gave me the little statue so that I may pray for Cuba. I have the little statue still in front of me on my desk.

May 31

My God, it is of my own free will, and with the help of your love, that I want to remain here in the streets with the poor to accomplish your will. I do not want to go back; my community is the poor; their security, mine; their health, my health.

My house is the house of the poor. Not simply the poor but the poorest of the poor.

Of the ones which we do not approach because we fear the dirt and infections.

Of the ones full of sickness and contagion.

Of the ones who cannot pray in churches because of the want of a piece of cloth.

Of the ones unable to eat because they have lost the strength to nourish themselves.

Of the ones unable to cry because they have shed all tears.

Of the ones lying on the street's pavement knowing they are about to die while all others go by uncaring and uninterested.

Of the ones needing not so much a house of bricks but an understanding heart.

Of the ones not so much in need of food but rather hungry for God's word.

Of the ones not so much wanting a cover for their nakedness but dignity, purity, justice.

Of the ones rejected, unwanted, unloved, fallen

along the way because they, too, are the poorest, the spiritually poorest of the poor, under whose distress, you, my God, disguise yourself, thirsting for my love the same as you do under the bread of the Eucharist.

Teach me how to recognize you in them and totally surrender to you today and every day until the end of my time, when again I will see you face to face in glory. Amen.

JUNE 1

During this month of June we shall have the opportunity of thanking and praising God for his great love for each one of us, through the preparation for the feast of the Sacred Heart of Jesus.

The Sacred Heart reveals to us the depth and height and breadth of God's compassionate, merciful love for each of us. Let us spend this month in deeper awareness of God's presence abiding within us, living within us, and making us true witnesses in the world of today.

JUNE 2

Our Lord says: "Come to me all you who are heavy burdened and I will give you rest." He is gentle and you are supposed to be gentle carriers of his love, apostles of the Sacred Heart. When you make a mistake, it is forgiven and forgotten when you bring it to the Sacred Heart. Go to the altar of God and try to be alone with him as much as possible so that you can hear him when he speaks in the silence of your heart.

JUNE 3

On June 3, 1977, Cardinal Poletti, Vicar of Rome, offered Holy Mass and gave the crosses to six men who would form a pious association, a contemplative group like the one I started in New York last year for the sisters.*They will both have the same constitution, the same life. All together we complete the unity of bread and wine.

Know the Word of God.

Love the Word of God.

Live the Word of God.

Give the Word of God and the Word of God will make you holy.

This association, initially called "Brothers of the Word," has now become "Missionaries of Charity Third Order M.C.III.O." or "Universal Fraternity of the Word." Mother revised the statutes of the association May 31, 1996. They are listed as an appendix at the back of this book.

JUNE 4

The heart of Jesus, pierced for love, reminds us of the great opportunity we have to receive the Body of Christ and his precious blood each day in the Eucharist. The heart of Jesus has been wounded by uncharitable acts. The heart of Jesus has been pierced by our failures.

Our Lord told St. Margaret Mary Alacoque, who fostered devotion to the Sacred Heart, that what hurt him most was to be neglected by those whom he has chosen as his own. We are the ones who neglect him when we fail to love.

JUNE 5

To become a saint one must suffer much and to love much we must suffer more. Suffering begets love, but it is also fruitful because it begets life for souls. How full of love we must be in order to be true to our name.

JUNE 6

A Jesuit priest told me about the time he was given a change of assignment. He spent the day on the train very happily moving to the new mission. When he got into the station, however, there was a telegram directing him to change trains and go to another mission. I asked him how he felt about that, if it was all right with him. He said that he accepted the change as the will of God, without question.

This is total surrender and complete obedience. When we belong to Jesus, he has the right to use us. Total surrender and complete obedience are the same thing.

JUNE 7

In giving us a new commandment, Jesus tells us that we must love the Lord our God with our whole heart, our whole mind, and our whole strength and our neighbor as ourselves. We must love our neighbor with that completeness with which we love God. Jesus didn't use a lot of words to make us understand how to love our neighbor. He simply said, "Love one another as I have loved you." We gladly serve people outside our home but we haven't the time to smile at those who are right here.

JUNE 8

There, in the heart of Jesus, nothing can separate you from the love of Christ and from love for each other. As much as possible, be alone with God so that you can listen to him. He will speak in the silence of your heart.

JUNE 9

God calls us to obedience not to torture us but to open our hearts to hear the word of God spoken through another creature. Christ tenderly calls us to unite our will to his love. Therefore, when I obey, I am not alone. If you look at your superior, you see only your superior. But if you look above, you will see the Lord. Jesus said again and again, "I have come to do the will of my Father." Your superior may be making a mistake in commanding you but if you say, "Be it done unto me according to your word," then your obedience, your spirit of sacrifice, will protect you.

JUNE 10

More and more, make your homes places of love and peace. Don't let the devil cheat you by his evil ways, tempting you to be unkind and harsh to one another. Enjoy each other. Love one another as Jesus has loved you. "See how they love each other," Jesus said. Let us be faithful to his teaching. Do not spoil the work of God by your unkindness.

How can you love Jesus in others unless you love him in your own family? We must make a real effort to make our families one heart of love. This is really the sign of Jesus with us.

JUNE 11

The heart of Jesus is an open heart. Spend your time there.

JUNE 12

Let us thank Jesus for all his goodness to us. Let us make a special point of giving others a living example of charity. We must unite in getting rid of all uncharitable remarks, thoughts, and actions. Then the Sacred Heart of Jesus will find in us true consolation and reparation for sin.

Let us spread devotion to the Sacred Heart at home and among others. Let us renew with great determination our offering to become apostles of the Sacred Heart, learning from the heart of Jesus how to be meek and humble.

JUNE 13

We fail to become holy because we are not completely united to Jesus, we do not have that love and zeal for holiness. We want to be holy but something holds us back, perhaps something small. Ask him for the strength to become really holy. The person who doesn't hurt others through speech, through the tongue, is already holy. To be holy is nothing special, it is simply our duty.

JUNE 14

Do not let the past disturb you—just bury everything in the Sacred Heart and begin again with joy. Make a real effort to grow in true love, reparation, and forgiveness. Try to make your home a place where Our Lord can come and rest for awhile with you.

Jesus has promised to write in his heart all those who spread devotion to his Sacred Heart. Jesus cannot deceive us—our names are written in his heart. Let us ask one very special grace from the Sacred Heart: Love for Our Lady through all the work we do for Jesus, with Jesus, and to Jesus. Ask him to deepen our love so that it is more personal and intimate.

JUNE 15

I pray that you will understand the words of Jesus, "Love one another as I have loved you." Ask yourself, "How has he loved me? Do I really love others in the same way?" Unless this love is among us, we can kill ourselves with work and it will only be work, not love. Work without love is slavery.

JUNE 16

Don't search for Jesus in far lands—he is not there. He is close to you; he is with you. Just keep the lamp burning and you will always see him. Keep on filling the lamp with all these little drops of love, and you will see how sweet is the Lord you love.

JUNE 17

In all community difficulties, you must become as a living tabernacle of God most high, as the holy family was at Nazareth. When you are tempted to respond to difficulty in bitterness and temper, touch the cross that you carry on the left side, close to your heart. Say, "Passion of Christ, strengthen me." Never lower yourself to become like the Pharisees who wanted to kill Christ.

JUNE 18

When we give free service to the poor, the word "free" reminds us that we must depend on Divine Providence. Freely we have received, now freely we give. That means we do not have government grants, we are not maintained by the church, we have no salary. That is why we must protect that word "free." We can't allow people to take it from us, to spoil it. We must keep everything simple, not demanding extra or unnecessary things.

JUNE 19

We have nothing to fear, not even the devil. But one virtue the devil fears most is humility. He is terrified more by humility than deep faith because humility is the virtue that makes us like Jesus. Jesus asked us to learn from him because, he said, "I am meek and humble of heart." We should try to learn from Jesus himself rather than relying on books. If we try to learn humility from books we become confused and it seems difficult to imitate the way of humility.

JUNE 20

Once, when I was traveling, I went from house to house for ten straight days. In the morning I would wake up and wonder, "Where am I?" It was a big sacrifice but joy came with that total surrender. Our total surrender consists in being completely available to God and to the church. Your superior can change your job and your companions, not due to personal likes but for the glory of God. You may be the only one in the house and so again, you clean the toilet. You must not kill your feelings when things like this happen but you must offer them as a sacrifice. This is the cross you have to bear.

JUNE 21

How tenderly Jesus speaks when he gives himself to us in Holy Communion. "My flesh is meat indeed and my blood is drink indeed. He who eats my flesh and drinks my blood lives in me and I in him." Oh, what could Jesus do more than give us his flesh for food? No, no one could do more or show a greater love for us.

JUNE 22

Criticism is nothing less than dressed up pride. It eats up all the love of God. A truly generous soul must never stoop to criticism. As a rule, people who criticize never do it openly, but go about doing it in a whisper. Refrain from prejudice, which means to set your mind against somebody. It is very sad when it becomes a part of our lives.

JUNE 23

A day alone with Jesus will spur us on to vigorous pursuit of holiness through personal love for him. Jesus desires our perfection with unspeakable ardor. Scripture says, "This is the will of God, your sanctification." Jesus' Sacred Heart is filled with an insatiable longing to see us advance toward holiness. To do this, we must continually practice the love of God.

JUNE 24

In your visits to the homes of our people, encourage true devotion to the Sacred Heart and the family rosary. Encourage the Catholic families to be consecrated to the Sacred Heart and to the Immaculate Heart of Mary. See that they have a holy picture, however small, in their homes. Strive to keep families together, remembering the saying, "The family that prays together, stays together." There are many broken homes but our work is to bring Jesus to the poor and to show them how to bring everything to him in prayer. If a family needs more help, take the time to settle the problem even if you must repeatedly seek the assistance of the parish priest.

JUNE 25

Be faithful in little things for in them lies our strength. To the good God, nothing is little. He is so great and we are so small but he stoops down and sends those little things to us to give us the chance to prove our love for him. Since he makes them, they are very great, they are infinite. So be faithful in little practices of love for they will build within you a life of holiness and make you Christlike.

JUNE 26

When we fail to practice penance, very soon a love of luxury creeps into our hearts. We start to make excuses for ourselves and become less generous as the spirit of penance relaxes. Penance holds a very special place in our Society. Through it, we expiate our faults, make the body more submissive to the will, and obtain abundant graces. The saints did many great penances. We are not called to the extraordinary ones but to the small daily ones that draw the soul to God and God to the soul.

June 27

Do not have long discussions on prayer. Learn from Jesus how to pray and allow him to pray in you and through you. Then put the fruit of that prayer into living action by loving one another as Jesus loves you.

June 28

Jesus taught us to pray: "Pray like this: 'Our Father … thy will be done … forgive us as we forgive….'" It is so simple yet so beautiful. It comes throughout the day, on every day of our lives. If we pray the "Our Father" and live it, we will know holiness. Everything is there: God, myself, my neighbor.

June 29

In the name of Jesus and for the love of Jesus and because Jesus has said that anything we ask you in his name will be granted, grant me the grace to love you above all, the grace of making my heart like the heart of Jesus, meek and humble.

This is how Cardinal O'Connor, Archbishop of New York, met and became a good friend of Mother Teresa:

"It was at my Episcopal Consecration in St. Peter's Basilica of Rome. During the recessional, I noticed a woman dressed in a strange way, half hidden by a column. As I approached her, attracted by her presence, but before I could speak anything to her, she said, 'Give him permission. Give him permission to use you, without consulting you.'"

It was this simple sentence spoken by Mother Teresa to Cardinal O'Connor that created a bond of trust between them that lasted for Mother until her death.

JULY 1

This being the month of the Precious Blood, increase your love for Holy Mass and the passion of Christ by accepting with joy all the little sacrifices that come daily. Do not bypass the small gifts for they are very precious for yourself and for others. During this month, we shall often pray this prayer: "In union with all the Masses being offered throughout the world, I offer you my heart. Make it meek and humble like yours."

JULY 2

Are you bound so closely with Jesus that nothing can separate you from him? Can Jesus be united with the Father in your heart? Are you so recollected, so pure, so easy within that he can pray with the Father in your heart? Remember, prayer is difficult if you have no silence of the heart because it is there that God speaks. Then you will be able to speak from the fullness of your heart.

Remember three things: total surrender to God, loving trust with each other, joy with all. Then you will be holy like Jesus. Holiness is joy, love, compassion, and especially, humility. A person who is humble and pure is on the way to great holiness. Just as pride cannot enter holiness, so humiliations lead to holiness. True friendship can help you lead a life of holiness. Everything should be directed toward your growth in holiness but remember, no one is going to force you to be holy.

In our hearts, we all crave to be something to someone. Our vow of chastity is a means to this, a means to be something to Jesus. It is more than simply not getting married. Many people choose not to get married because they want to experience the fruit of chastity. So what is chastity in our lives? It is hunger for God.

July 5

Do not be afraid to be poor and so proclaim his poverty. The sisters in Rome built a house just like the people's. They became first-class builders but since the house is only a barrack, it didn't take much time. This living example of poverty has been a great grace for our barrack people and for others.

We are not forced to be poor but we choose to be poor for the love of Jesus. Christ, being rich, became poor for us.

July 6

Let us go very close to God's heart and renew our commitment to chastity.

With St. Maria Goretti we must say that we would rather die than sin. Often during the day we should pray: "Purity of the Heart of Jesus, purify my heart. In union with all the Precious Blood being offered in the sacrifice of the Mass throughout the world, I offer you my heart for all my brothers and sisters, especially the ones who are tempted to sin against purity."

Unless you become like a little child, you cannot enter into heaven. And what is being a little child? It is having a clean heart, a pure heart, a heart that holds Jesus.

It is said that humility is truth and Jesus is truth, therefore, the one thing that will make us most Christlike is humility. Hiding the gifts God has given you or doing your work in an inefficient way is not humility.

Say this little prayer often: "Jesus, you said that anything we ask in your name will be granted. Therefore, in your name and for love of you, I ask you to grant me the grace to love you only, the grace to make my heart like yours, meek and humble."

If we deliberately allow venial sin to become a daily bread, a moral anemia, the soul becomes weak all around, the spiritual life begins to crumble and fall apart. God preserve us from any deliberate sin, no matter how small it may be. Nothing is small when it means going against God.

July 10

Superiors may make a mistake in commanding but we are infallible in obeying.

July 11

In our novitiate house in Rome we have a big beautiful vine, spread out, covering the whole place. One day I told the novices to take the Gospel of St. John, chapter fifteen as their meditation. They went out, each one sitting under the vine, feeling, touching the vine, reading the Gospel again and again.

One of the novices gave me this lesson: "Mother, there was not even one grape on the vine but all of the grapes were on the branches. The branches are full of fruit, and it is so strange that there is nothing on the vine itself. See how our lives are so connected, we are the branches and we are supposed to bear fruit."

We, being his love, must bear fruit of compassion, love, and concern for one another and the people with whom we work.

July 12

Jesus was sent to bring the Good News to the world, to the poor. How strange then that he spent thirty years in Nazareth. Even the Jews thought nothing of it. What good can come out of Nazareth? Even Mary must have wondered when Jesus would begin his work.

Our first great responsibility is to be a family, a community, revealing first to one another something of God's own love and concern and tenderness. "See how they love one another." Being so close to each other it is possible to miss God's love and goodness that is to be found in those who are so near to us. We need to help each other to forget the everyday deficiencies and to start a new life every day in the joy of Jesus.

Jesus wants to tell you again and again how much is the love he has for each one of you. I worry that some of you still have not really met Jesus one to one, you and Jesus alone, not from books but from being with him in your heart.

Until you can hear Jesus in the silence of your own heart, you will not be able to hear him saying "I thirst" in the heart of the poor.

July 15

We must be convinced that nothing adorns a human soul with greater splendor than the virtue of chastity and nothing defiles a human soul more than the opposite vice. Yet the glory of chastity is not in immunity from temptation—it is in victory over temptations. A chaste person is not free from temptations but overcomes them.

July 16

We must be the light of charity. Charity and humility are twins born of sanctity.

July 17

God has shown his greatness by using nothingness. Let us give God free hand to use us without consulting us. Let us accept whatever he gives and give whatever he takes with a big smile!

JULY 18

The Gospel needs to be brought back to the countries falling away from Christianity. Bring the word to the hungry and thirsting for God, starting with your own family. Charity begins at home.

JULY 19

Jesus is the hungry one. I believe that God is hungrier for our love than we are for his love. He is hungrier to give his love than we are to receive.

JULY 20

Somebody asked me: what is prayer? For me, prayer is that oneness with God.

JULY 21

All we do is but a drop in the ocean, but if we do not do it, the ocean will be one drop less.

July 22

If our houses are real communities of love and union we will overcome hatred. Love begins at home. Everything depends on how we love each other. Do not be afraid to love until it hurts because this is how Jesus loved. Much of the hurt in our homes comes from uncontrolled use of words, said anywhere, in front of other people. Let us open our eyes to the harm we do.

July 23

Surrender is the only thing that is our own.

July 24

Our holy faith is nothing but a gospel of love. It reveals to us God's love for us and in return our love for God, who is love. A missionary must be a missionary of love. We must spread God's love on earth in order to help souls repent wholeheartedly from sin. Strengthen others against temptation, increase their generosity, reinforce their desire to suffer for Christ.

Let us "act" Christ's love among mankind, remembering the words of the *Imitation of Christ,* which tells us that love feels no burden, values no labors, would willingly do more than it can, and doesn't complain of impossibilities because it perceives that it can do all things. When weary, love is not tired; when strained, love is not constrained; when frightened, love is not disturbed. Like a living flame, like a torch on fire, love mounts upward and securely passes through all opposition.

JULY 25

Thoughtfulness is the beginning of great sanctity. If you learn the art of thoughtfulness you will become more and more Christlike. His heart was meek and he always thought of the needs of others. Our vocation, to be beautiful, must be full of thought for others. Jesus went about doing good. Our Lady did nothing else at Cana but think of the needs of others and make those needs known to Jesus. The thoughtfulness of Mary and Joseph was so great that it made Nazareth the abode of the Most High.

JULY 26

Prayer is as necessary as the air, as the blood in our bodies, as anything to keep us alive—to keep us alive to the grace of God.

JULY 27

Silence can never be corrected. Very often, I have the answer but I don't give it, I wait, and I am grateful to God for giving me the opportunity because silence can never be corrected.

Let us make a resolution to control our tongues. If we are to love Jesus with undivided love in our brothers and sisters and in the poor, then our tongues must be clean. Each day, Jesus comes on our tongues in the Eucharist. When I was a child, my mother told me in preparation for first Holy Communion that if I told a lie my tongue would turn black. One day, I told a lie and ran to the looking glass to see! It might have been my imagination, but I am sure I saw that my tongue was black. And I went and told my mother about the lie. I must take care that my tongue does not get dirty because Jesus will rest there as he rested in the womb of his mother, Mary.

JULY 28

Are you really living all for Jesus? Are your ears, your eyes, your heart only all for Jesus? Spend time alone with Jesus. He has called you, you belong to him, and he will give you his heart to love him if you ask.

My sister and I used to read the same books. One day my sister read a book and passed it to me. As soon as I read two pages, I felt it would be a sin to read that book. Later I asked my sister whether she had read the book. She replied that she had and had found nothing wrong in it. There was no sin in my sister reading the book, but in conscience I could not read it.

It was her humility that drew God to Mary. She was so free because she was so poor. She was so pure, so full of grace that God could use her very life to give life to his Son, Jesus. God used her flesh and blood to form the body and blood of Jesus. This body and blood he poured out from the cross as a redeeming means of forgiveness and greater love. And something very wonderful happened as the last drop of blood mingled with the water from his wounded heart: His last thought was for his mother, that she would have someone to love her. Jesus gave her to John, his beloved, to take his place. John, in his love for Jesus, took her to be his own mother.

Could Jesus, during the sacrifice of the Mass, say the same to us: "Behold, your mother"? Is our love so tender, our heart so pure, that we could take her to ourselves as John did? At every Mass, we, too, have the chance to take her as our own. We need only believe. When we receive Jesus in Holy Communion, let us ask her to come to us and teach us how to take care of him as she did at Nazareth. We have a beautiful opportunity to take care of him in the poor and to be real contemplatives at the heart of the world.

July 31

Cardinal Poletti, the Vicar for the Diocese of Rome, was asked by Pope John Paul II to look for an empty house which would fit Mother Teresa's project of providing for unwed mothers. The pope said to the cardinal, half seriously, half jokingly, "When you find it, be sure to bring me the key, otherwise she will not believe me."

The house, later opened at Primavalle, a section of Rome, has a picture of the Holy Father at the entrance giving the key to Mother Teresa.

It was this determination of such a humble nun that allowed her, at the time of her death, to have opened 602 houses in 125 countries with 3,914 sisters, for the service of the poorest of the poor, materially and spiritually alike. Providing shelter for the homeless, unwanted babies, lepers, alcoholics, addicts, prostitutes, AIDS patients, dying, the deviant and dejected of all sorts. Her work is now carried out around the world by several branches of her religious society of the Missionaries of Charity she had founded at different stages of her life: sisters, brothers, priests, and lay persons, including the Missionaries of Charity Third Order. Some of these branches are active, some contemplative.

AUGUST 1

The feast of the Immaculate Heart of Mary, cause of our joy, is drawing near. Our preparation for the great day should be that of deep, humble gratitude to God. Let us ask two special graces from Our Lady: The grace of perseverance in our beautiful vocation, and delicate love for God's poor. The greatness of Our Lady was in her humility. No wonder Jesus wanted to live so close to her. We learn from him and from her one lesson: To be meek and humble of heart.

AUGUST 2

When you first come to know Jesus, you learn how to pray. When you pray, stand straight. When you pray, your vocation is strong. When you pray, you begin to love. When your prayer diminishes, your vocation is in great danger.

AUGUST 3

Jesus was fully confident but in the eyes of the world, he was zero. They asked, how can he preach? Is he not the carpenter's son? Even the cross was a sign of failure. Yet the salvation of the whole world was entrusted to him. Mary must have wondered: When? Why? How?

You and I are here for what? For the salvation and sanctification of the poorest of the poor. Just by washing that leper, teaching those few children, doing small things for and with Jesus—that is saving and sanctifying action. Yes, it is the love that does it.

AUGUST 4

Humility always radiates the glory and greatness of God. How wonderful are the ways of God who used humility, smallness, helplessness, and poverty to prove his love to the world. Do not be afraid to be humble, small, and helpless in order to prove your love for God.

August 5

When I first went to the slums to teach catechism to the children, I asked a little four-year-old child, Nironjon, "Can you tell me about the Blessed Trinity?"

"The Blessed Trinity is like my finger," he said. "See, there are three parts. Each part separately does not make a finger but only the three parts together make one."

August 6

What is this dependence on Divine Providence? A firm and lively faith that God can and will help us. That he can is evident because he is almighty. That he will is certain because he promises to help in so many passages of Holy Writ and because he is infinitely faithful to all his promises.

August 7

Jesus' way of poverty was simple. He trusted his Father completely.

AUGUST 8

Love God generously, with trust, without looking back, without fear. Give yourself fully to Jesus. He will use you to accomplish great things if you believe much more in his love than in your weakness. Believe in him, trust him with blind and absolute confidence because he is Jesus.

AUGUST 9

Receive forgiveness to give forgiveness.

AUGUST 10

What does it mean for us to be the poorest of the poor? Do we know what it means to be hungry and thirsty, lonely and unloved? Do we know what it means to be sick and unwanted, homeless and misunderstood? Do the poor really know us? Do they love us? Are they happy in our presence? Let us renew our love for the poor. We will be able to do so only if we are faithful to the poverty we have chosen.

August 11

Grumbling is a hidden devil. It is something highly contagious. It's like a mosquito bite—the sting is there and after a few months you get malaria.

August 12

Our sisters are working in New York with the shut-ins. What they see—the terrible pain of our people, that loneliness, that fear, that feeling of being alone, unwanted, unloved. I think that it is much greater than even cancer and AIDS. The sisters have met people like that very often—completely brokenhearted, desperate with big feelings of hurt. You may meet people like that and you must come to know them. You must come to know your children, and very often we find this in our own communities—brothers and sisters who feel that kind of feeling. Do we know the pain and poverty of our people with whom we come in contact?

August 13

Let Jesus use you without consulting you. Obedience is natural if I realize that I belong to Jesus.

Eve of the Feast of the Assumption

O heart of Mary, heart of the tenderest of mothers, cause of our joy, we consecrate ourselves unreservedly to you, our hearts, our bodies, our souls. We desire to belong to you in life and in death. You know, O Immaculate Mother, that your divine Son has chosen us in his infinite mercy, in spite of our misery and sinfulness, not only as his children and his spouses but also as his victims to console his divine heart in the sacrament of his love, to atone for sacrileges and to obtain pardon for poor sinners.

We come today to offer him, through your most pure heart, the entire sacrifice of ourselves. Of our own free choice, we renounce all the desires and inclinations of our corrupt nature and we accept willingly and lovingly whatever sufferings he may be pleased to send us. But conscious of our weakness we implore you, O Holy Mother, to shield us with your maternal protection and to obtain from your divine son all the graces we need to persevere.

Bless this house and each soul confided to our care, our relations, friends, and benefactors, that all may persevere in grace or recover it if lost. When the hour of death comes, may our hearts, modeled on your Iimmaculate Heart, breathe forth their last sign into the heart of your divine Son. Amen.

AUGUST 15

Assumption of Our Lady Into Heaven

And Mary said, "Yes," at that moment he came to her heart. What happened then? She who was so small became great to let him live and love in her.

AUGUST 16

Prayer cannot live by itself: it cannot be prayer unless it is fed by sacrifices.

AUGUST 17

Our vocation is Jesus. Scripture says very clearly: "I have called you by name, you are precious to me. Water will not drown you, fire will not burn you. I will give nations for you, you are precious. How could a mother forget her infant, be without tenderness for the child of her womb? Even if these forget, I will never forget you. You are precious to me, carried in the palm of my hand."

Think about your homes. You grew up with your brothers and sisters, praying together, raised by the same parents. What happened? Why are you here? You must have heard Jesus call your name. St. Margaret Mary says that Jesus told her: "My love for you is not a joke." So too, our love for Jesus is not a joke. We have said, "Yes, I come." We must have that conviction that he has called us by name, that we belong to him, and that nothing and nobody can separate us from him.

AUGUST 18

Our Blessed Mother calls us to fast and do penance and pray. Let us be faithful to these things if we are sincere in our desire to bring souls to Jesus. Pray, fast, and do penance for priests, to help them be holy and bring souls to Jesus.

AUGUST 19

Be faithful to Christ! Pray for perseverance! Remember that you have been created for greater things. Never stoop lower than that ideal. Let nothing satisfy you but God.

AUGUST 20

St. Bernard, in his commentary on the Canticle of Canticles, says: "Pay attention to the little foxes that sneak in after us, destroying the vines in flower."

We may carry water upstairs for a bath and find three buckets already full in our bathing room. Then the temptation comes to use all the water. If you have to sleep in a corner where there is no breeze, do not gasp and pant to show how much you feel it. In these little things, you can practice poverty. Poverty makes us free. That is why we can joke and smile and have a happy heart for Jesus.

August 21

The greatest offering we can make is that of a fervent heart. If you really want to be a true co-worker of Christ, keep the rule of the Society. We are consecrated to him; Jesus has chosen us for himself. What joy is ours because we are always in close contact with Christ in the distressing disguise of the poor.

August 22

Feast of the Missionaries of Charity

May Mary be a mother to each of us, the cause of our joy. May we be Jesus to her, the cause of her joy. No one has learned humility as Mary did. The handmaid of the Lord was completely empty of self and God filled her with grace, with himself. To be a handmaid means to be at someone's disposal, to be used according to someone's wishes. It means to belong to someone without reserve, with full trust and joy. Our Lady was a willing handmaid of the Lord. Cheerfulness and joy were her strength.

When we think of the name of our society—The Missionaries of Charity—we should feel a little remorse of conscience if our charity, both inside and outside the community, is not what it should be. Our charity should be full of humility, simplicity, openness, generosity, forgiveness, and thoughtfulness. In general, we should improve our politeness, understanding, brotherly love, maturity, and our deep faith in one another.

My secret is simple—I pray.

Scripture says: "Make my joy complete by your unanimity, possessing the one love, united in spirit and ideals. Never act out of rivalry or conceit; rather, let all parties think humbly of others as superior to themselves, each of you looking to others' interests rather than to his own."

Without this union of family spirit, the Society could scarcely continue to exist. Certainly it could not accomplish the task for which it was founded. The greatest assistance we can render our community is the faithful observance of this law of charity which is also the life of every family. On the other hand, the greatest enemies of a community, of a family, are those who by their uncharitableness stir up disunion.

August 26

Everything depends on how we love each other.

August 27

We must "pray the work," be souls of prayer right in the midst of the slums, praying the work with Jesus, for Jesus, to Jesus. Someone has promoted the idea that our vocal prayer together is not prayer. I am sure that Mary and Jesus prayed the psalms together often. Naturally, if we only say prayers, mindlessly, we might not be praying. To pray the prayer means to be completely united to Jesus in such a way as to allow him to pray in us, with us, for us, through us.

August 28

St. Augustine tells us that progress in holiness depends on God and myself—on God's grace and on my will. Each of us must have a true and living resolution to reach holiness. If we are faithful in little practices of love, in little sacrifices, in little interior mortifications, then we will become more Christlike and build within ourselves the life of holiness. Holiness is only a very high degree of love. Let us all unite in helping each other to become holy.

We must reach the heart. To reach the heart, we must do—love is proven in deeds. People are attracted more by what they see than by what they hear. Therefore, our sisters should not spend their time in meetings and committees. If people wish to help, let them come and see. The reality is more attractive than the abstract idea. Try to put into the hearts of your older children a love for home. Make them long to be with their families. So much sin could be avoided if people really loved their home.

Blessed are they that are hungry:
  for God's love
  for the Bread of Life
  for human love
  for holiness
  for a life of prayer
  for respect and human dignity
  for recognition as a child of God
  for a word of sympathy, for a smile
Do I recognize these hungers?
In the hunger of my loneliness, where do I turn?
In the hunger of my sinfulness, is Jesus my first thought?
Is Jesus the hunger of my life?
Is Jesus the deepest love in my life?

August 31

Mother Teresa asked Pope John Paul II, as she was leaving an audience one time, "Holy Father, pray that I may not spoil the work." The pope in a quick response replied, "And you, Mother, pray that I may not spoil the church!"

SEPTEMBER 1

During this month of September, as we celebrate four feasts of our Lady [8th-Birthday, 12th-Name of Mary, 15th-Sorrow, 24th-Compassion], let us learn from her: humility, purity, sharing, and thoughtfulness. We will then, like Mary, become holy people, being able to look up and see only Jesus; our light and example will be only Jesus; and we will be able to spread his fragrance everywhere we go. We will flood our souls with his Spirit and so in us, through us, and with us glorify the Father.

SEPTEMBER 2

What we are trying to do is to bring Jesus to the poor and the poor to Jesus. That is all we are trying to do.

SEPTEMBER 3

We become religious to witness to the high holiness of the church. By approving our congregation, the church expects much from us. The church believes that our way of life will lead many to holiness. If we live our vows fully, this life has the power to bring us to perfect love, to make us holy, to help us love God perfectly. We may make mistakes but that love for one another and for Jesus must remain.

SEPTEMBER 4

Our Lord has a very special love for the chaste. His own mother and St. Joseph and St. John, the beloved disciple, were chaste. We desire to be chaste because we belong to Jesus Christ, Son of the Living God. We want to be chaste because of the work we do as co-workers of Christ. Our chastity must be so pure that it draws the most impure to the Sacred Heart of Christ.

SEPTEMBER 5

Today is the anniversary of Mother Teresa's death in 1997. The following quotation is taken from a general letter she wrote on the day of her death:

"Stand near Our Lady to listen to the thirst of Jesus and to answer with your whole heart."

Once you begin to neglect obedience, one by one everything goes. It can happen to any one of us. Obedience is difficult but that's where love comes from. There are so many broken families because a woman will not obey a man and a man will not obey a woman.

We belong to Jesus and obedience is our strength. You must do small acts of obedience with great love. Obedience is not a joke, it is a sacrifice. The more you love God, the more you will obey. Obedience is a cross—pick up your cross and follow him. Everyone in the world has to obey in some way or another. People are forced to obey or they will lose their jobs. But we obey out of love for Jesus.

Never stop to do anything secretly. Hiding is the beginning of lying, lie in action.

SEPTEMBER 8

Obedience, well lived, frees us from selfishness and pride and helps us to find God. In him, we find the whole world. Obedience is a special grace that produces unfailing peace, inward joy, and close union with God. Obedience lived with joy creates a deep awareness of his presence. Fidelity to obedience—constant, prompt, cheerful, undivided obedience—becomes like drops of oil that keep the light of Jesus living in our life. Our Lady will teach us how to obey like Jesus, who was obedient unto death.

SEPTEMBER 9

Immaculate Heart of Mary, our Queen and Mother, be more and more our way to Jesus, the light of Jesus, and the life of Jesus in each one of us. In return for this gift, let us be more and more a cause of joy to one another, the way of peace to one another, and the living love of Jesus for one another.

Today is Inspiration Day, the day on which our Society was born. You can show your gratitude and give me a great gift by speaking and thinking well of each other, appreciating the good other sisters are doing, and accepting each other as you are. Always meet each other with a smile.

You have given your best and because of your trust and loyalty, we have been able to go forward without fear or hesitation. Let us all be one heart, full of love. Let us allow Jesus to live his life in each one of us to the full.

We see the humility of Jesus:

In the crib;

In the exile of Egypt;

In the hidden life at Nazareth;

In his inability to make people understand him;

In the desertion of his apostles;

In the dislike of the scribes and Pharisees;

In the terrible sufferings of his Passion and death;

In his permanent state of humility in the tabernacle.

SEPTEMBER 12

I like these words, "Mary went in haste." Mary is not only our mother, but our way to Jesus. See what Mary said at the wedding: "Do what he tells you." Jesus can and will do great things if we do what he tells us. Obedience is not meant to be a torture or that I have to do it, but it is meant to be a joy. Our Lady's name is mentioned only twelve times in the New Testament and nowhere does it say that God spoke directly to her, even when the greatest possible thing was to happen in the world. God used a creature, an angel, to speak to her.

SEPTEMBER 13

If we are faithful, humble, holy, and dedicated to serving the poor, the others will learn from us. But let us examine ourselves to see what they are learning. Do they see our efforts to belong wholly to God, even in our failures? Do they see our efforts to be holy like Jesus and humble like Mary? If we really obey, we are holy. Our Lady was so holy, so full of grace because she lived her surrender, "Be it done unto me according to your word."

Jesus has the same tenderness for each of you that he had for his apostles at the Last Supper. You are preparing for your final surrender—to become professed Missionaries of Charity—and you will be giving your "yes" to your own crucifixion. The last thing we do at night is to kiss the cross. The first thing we do in the morning is to kiss the cross. Jesus is asking each of you to accept whatever he gives and give whatever he takes with a big smile.

Mary has much to teach us about humility. She was full of grace, yet she was only the handmaid of the Lord. She was the Mother of God yet served as a handmaid in the house of Elizabeth. She was immaculately conceived yet she humbly met Jesus, himself humiliated, carrying his cross. Near the cross she stood as one of us, a sinner needing redemption.

Like her, great are the graces we have received. Like her, let us always accept the cross in whatever way it comes. Like her, let us with grace and delicacy touch the lonely and unwanted. Like her, let us not be ashamed or slow to do humble works.

Humility of the heart of Mary, fill my heart. Teach me, as you taught Jesus, to be meek and humble of heart and so to glorify the Father.

SEPTEMBER 16

Penance calls us away from sin and to God. It leads us away from mediocrity and to a life of fervor, generosity, and sanctity. Contemplation is impossible without asceticism and self-abnegation, without a sharing in the passion of Christ, in the suffering of the poorest of the poor. We must give up sin, our past self-indulgence, and practice more intense self-sacrificing love for him.

SEPTEMBER 17

The joy of the Lord is our strength. Therefore, each of us will accept a life of poverty in cheerful trust. We will offer cheerful obedience from our inward joy. We will minister to Christ in the distressing disguise of the poor with cheerful devotion. If our work is done with joy, we will have no reason to be unhappy.

SEPTEMBER 18

Cardinal Newman wrote: "Help me to spread your fragrance wherever I go.... Let me preach you without preaching, not by words but by my example, by the catching force, the sympathetic influence of what I do, the evident fullness of the love my heart bears for you." Our works of love are nothing but works of peace. Let us do them with greater love and efficiency.

We must obey the rule with a big, willing heart, faithful to the least detail. We must have a soul that has learned to see and love—even in the least prescriptions—the most holy will of God. We are faithful to the least things, not for their own sake but for the sake of the great things, that is, for the sake of the will of God. The smallest rule contains the will of God as much as the biggest rule. If we love Christ, we will live according to his will, according to the rules.

We must obey as Christ did, unto his death on the cross. He saw the will of God in everything and everybody and so he could say that he did the things that were pleasing to his Father. He obeyed Caiaphas and Pilate because their authority was given from above. He didn't look at their human limitations but submitted to them with obedience and dignity out of love for his Father.

If we obey like Jesus, our lives will be pleasing to God and he will say, "This is my beloved child in whom I am well pleased."

SEPTEMBER 20

The Holy Father spoke in one of his messages about peace, and one thing he said was this: "No to violence and yes to peace." What is violence? In the first place, we think of weapons, knives, killings. We never think of connecting violence with our tongues. But the first weapon, the most cruel weapon, is the tongue. Examine what part your tongue has played in creating peace or violence. We can really wound a person, we can kill a person, with our tongue.

SEPTEMBER 21

The most appealing invitation to embrace the religious life is the witness of our own lives, the spirit in which we react to our divine calling, the completeness of our dedication, the generosity and cheerfulness of our service to God, the love we have for one another, the apostolic zeal with which we witness to Christ's love for the poorest of the poor.

Jesus said to St. Paul: "Saul, Saul, why do you persecute me?" not "Why do you persecute the Christians?" This clarifies that we serve Christ in the poorest of the poor: "Whatsoever you do to the least of my brethren, you do to me."

Our vow clearly states that our service is wholehearted, not slapdash or halfhearted.

Penance is absolutely necessary. Nothing has greater effect in restraining the disordered passions of the soul and in subjecting the natural appetites to right reason. Through penance, we shall possess the heavenly joys which surpass the pleasures of earth as much as the soul surpasses the body and heaven surpasses the earth.

SEPTEMBER 24

The following quotation is from Mother Teresa's final letter written on the day of her death:

"Loving trust and total surrender made Our Lady say 'yes' to the message of the angel. And cheerfulness made her run in haste to serve her cousin Elizabeth. That is so much our life: saying 'yes' to Jesus and running in haste to serve him in the poorest of the poor. Let us keep very close to Our Lady and she will make that same spirit grow in each one of us."

SEPTEMBER 25

Jesus has chosen us to be souls of prayer. The value of our actions corresponds exactly to the value of our prayer. Our actions are fruitful only if they are the true expressions of earnest prayer.

Jesus wants us to be more childlike, more humble, more grateful in prayer. And we do not pray alone but with the knowledge that we belong to the mystical body of Christ, which is always praying. There is no such thing as isolated prayer but instead Jesus is praying in me and Jesus is praying with me. The body of Christ is always praying.

SEPTEMBER 26

You don't know how very happy I am to let God just do whatever he likes with me.

SEPTEMBER 27

Thoughtfulness and generosity come from a meek and humble heart. This is the contradiction of what the devil says: "I will not serve" and what Jesus says: "I have not come to be served, but to serve!"

SEPTEMBER 28

I can understand the greatness of God but I cannot understand his humility. It becomes so clear in him being in love with each one of us separately and completely. It is as if there is no one but me in the world. He loves me so much. Each one of us can say this with great conviction.

SEPTEMBER 29

Jesus was sent by the Father to give us the good news of our Father's love. When the time came for him to return to the Father, he left living proof of that love in the Eucharist. Look at the crucifix and look at the tabernacle. After giving us such great proof of this love and mercy by dying for us, why did Jesus give us the Eucharist? Surely the crucifixion would have been enough. But Jesus has given us the chance to share in his crucifixion, to continue it in our lives, to connect his suffering with his body in the Eucharist, resting in the tabernacle.

SEPTEMBER 30

The other day we went to Jamshedpore, to a big factory where they make parts for airplanes. In one corner a man was sitting and making little screws. I went near him and asked him what he was making. He looked up at me and said, "I am making an airplane." I said, "Airplane?" He said, "Yes, without these little screws, the plane will not move."

See the connection? Each one of us is important to the body of Christ, the church. Ask Jesus again and again to make you understand this.

When St. Thérèse, the Little Flower, was dying, the other sisters wondered what the superior would write about her in the little life story the convent sent out upon the death of each nun. She seemed so simple, so ordinary. Thérèse heard these questions and they made her happy. She said to Jesus: "You have done great things with nothingness." Thérèse had done small things with great love, done ordinary things with extraordinary love, and Rome made her a saint for that.

In the convent where the Little Flower lived, there was an old nun who was impossible to please. She was always grumbling and so no one wanted to take care of her. The Little Flower, out of love for Jesus, volunteered to assist her. Every day, the litany of complaints began: "You are too slow" or "You are too fast" or "What are you doing? You will kill me. Can't you go faster?" This elderly sister grumbled constantly but Thérèse obeyed her and did all she asked. The Little Flower's obedience was beautiful and complete because she wanted to be all for Jesus, her crucified Jesus, her spouse.

St. Bernadette entered the convent but her superior was jealous of her and asked: "Why did Our Lady choose to appear to you?" St. Bernadette never answered her superior rudely but obeyed her blindly. Nothing is foolish when done for God, out of love for Jesus.

OCTOBER 2

Holy angels, our advocates, pray for us.
Holy angels, our brothers, pray for us.
Holy angels, our counselors, pray for us.
Holy angels, our defenders, pray for us.
Holy angels, our enlighteners, pray for us.
Holy angels, our friends, pray for us.
Holy angels, our guides, pray for us.
Holy angels, our helpers, pray for us.
Holy angels, our intercessors, pray for us.

OCTOBER 3

Keep giving Jesus to people not by words but by example, by being in love with Jesus.

OCTOBER 4

Let us continue to say the prayer of St. Francis of Assisi every day. It is really helping us to come closer to each other.

Lord, make me an instrument of your peace;
where there is hatred let me sow love,
where there is injury let me sow pardon,
where there is doubt let me sow faith,
where there is despair let me give hope,
where there is darkness let me give light,
where there is sadness let me give joy.

O divine master, grant that I may
not try to be comforted but to comfort,
not try to be understood but to understand,
not try to be loved but to love.

Because it is in giving that we receive,
it is in forgiving that we are forgiven,
and it is in dying that we are born to eternal life.

OCTOBER 5

In order to pray, we need a pure heart so that we might be united with God. Mary's heart was clean, and so she was chosen by God and gave everything to God. We should pray: "Mary, Mother of Jesus, help me to make my heart pure. Be a mother to me now." She will help us to have a pure heart, to pray, and to be one with God.

OCTOBER 6

Humility and prayer—which will lead us to holiness—grow from a heart, mind, and tongue that live in silence with God. In that silence of the heart, God will speak.

Jesus asked his disciples to learn from him for he was meek and humble of heart. We, too, must be meek with one another and then we will be all right with God, humble with him, proving our love in wholehearted service.

OCTOBER 7

The rosary has been the strength of our Society from the very first days. Let us fervently and faithfully renew our devotion to this great prayer. In a special way, the Society owes its birth to the Immaculate Heart of Mary and its growth to her tender care. In return, let us thank her for what she has done for us and give her even greater love. Times have been joyful and hard for our Society, but together we have worked with Jesus and for Jesus, always aware that Mary, the cause of our joy, is by our side.

OCTOBER 8

Our first great responsibility is to be a family. We are to reveal first, to one another, something of God's own love and concern and tenderness. When others see us, they should say, "See how they love one another."

OCTOBER 9

If we love God with our whole soul, if we love Jesus Christ above all things, if we have tender love for Our Lady, we will be less inclined to be unduly attached to other creatures. Love for Jesus will produce these effects if it is intense, generous, and all-absorbing. It must fill our minds and hearts so that we no longer give a thought to human affection. If we do become entangled in ill-ordered affections, Jesus, who cannot suffer strange gods in our hearts, will reproach us severely.

OCTOBER 10

The suffering of the poor is very great throughout the world. We, too, are the poorest of the poor—but are we really poor? With poverty come freedom and charity. With charity comes a more intimate, personal love for Jesus. As we come to know each other better, knowledge will lead to love and love will lead to kind, joyful, peaceful service.

OCTOBER 11

Keep the joy of Jesus as your strength.

OCTOBER 12

Let Jesus use you without consulting you. Allow him to possess you so that you may possess him. But even in obedience, you have your will and God will not take your free will by force. He himself came to do the will of his Father and in Gethsemane, in spite of everything, said: "Not my will but yours be done."

OCTOBER 13

You must trust that our rule of life is the means of your sanctification, the weapon of your apostolate, the source of holiness, peace, and joy. It is a pledge of perseverance. Cling to the rule as a child clings to its mother.

OCTOBER 14

Contemplation is simply to realize God's constant presence and his tender love for us.

OCTOBER 15

Make an effort to radiate joy, which is the fruit of the Spirit and a characteristic mark of the kingdom of God. God is joy. We have no reason to be unhappy. Christ, wanting to share his joy with the disciples, prayed that "my joy may be in you and your joy be complete." Jesus must have radiated joy and you should do the same, in your eyes, attitude, the way you walk, the way you listen, and your whole being.

OCTOBER 16

Jesus was having a conversation with St. Gerard and he was saying, "Give me, give me." St. Gerard replied, "I have nothing to give you, I have given you everything." Jesus insisted: "Give me your sins."

OCTOBER 17

What is the connection between prayer and obedience? Prayer will give us a clean heart, a clean heart will help us to see God, and if we see God, we will obey. The more we pray, the better we will pray and that will produce the fruit of a clean heart. Singing hymns with brief verses and talking to God is prayer.

OCTOBER 18

To love, it is necessary to give.

To give, it is necessary to be free from selfishness, to have the courage of poverty.

OCTOBER 19

The greatest humility is to know that we are nothing, and this we come to know when we face God in prayer. It is only when we realize our nothingness, our emptiness, that God can fill us with himself.

OCTOBER 20

I'll never forget a young woman with four or five children who ran away from a good Catholic family. I couldn't understand. Her husband came to me and told me. I found her and asked her, "What has happened? You were such a good girl." This is what she said. "I was standing at my door the first time that man passed. The second time, I went to the door to see him. The third time, I looked out for him. The fourth time, he came inside."

The beginning was that little infidelity: "I never told my husband." In the same way, you cannot play with your undivided love for Christ.

OCTOBER 21

When we learn the need for silence and humility, we will have a better life of prayer. We should be professionals in prayer.

In reality, there is only one substantial prayer, Christ himself. Frequently, our prayers don't produce results because we fail to fix our minds and hearts on Christ. It is through him that our prayers can ascend to God. Often, a deep, fervent look at Christ makes the best prayer. We look at him and he looks at us.

OCTOBER 22

To almighty God, the smallest action given to him is great. But for us, we always measure how much we did, for how long. For God, there is no time. What should be important to us is how much love we put into the giving.

OCTOBER 23

Even God cannot fill what is full already. We must empty ourselves so that God can fill us.

OCTOBER 24

Our life of penance is one of renunciation and joy, deeply rooted in the mystery of the cross and resurrection. We joyfully embrace all the sacrifices involved in the fervent, generous living of our consecrated life in contemplation of God and in service to the poorest of the poor. We live in total surrender, loving trust, and cheerfulness, and we make fervent use of the sacrament of penance. We deny ourselves by fasting, abstinence, and by practicing restraint in the way we use things.

OCTOBER 25

Do others notice if you are absent? Do they miss your warmth, your presence? We should radiate the presence of Christ by our compassion. Do we fulfill this responsibility to be God's love and compassion in the world, in the community, in our family? Let us be his presence to others.

OCTOBER 26

If you do your work with joy, you can bring many souls to God. Joy is prayer, a sign of our generosity, evident in our eyes, our faces, our actions.

OCTOBER 27

When we neglect prayer, evil can penetrate our hearts. Ask yourself: Do I pray? How do I pray? How often do I pray? Do I feel the need to pray? When prayer is difficult, do I try to find a book that could help me? At those times, do I pray for a longer period of time and more frequently, with greater fidelity? Do I make up prayer that I have missed? Do I follow a method for meditation that will help me to pray? Do I have some small aspirations that I pray often? Both penance and aspirations will help us to grow in the spiritual life.

OCTOBER 28

To become holy, we need humility and prayer and all the spiritual and temporal gifts that God has given us. We will grow in holiness through love for one another, by sharing the joy of Jesus, and through sacrifice. Deepening our personal love for Our Lady will also help us become holy. We can do this especially by praying the rosary with ever greater understanding wherever we are, even when traveling. We will also grow in holiness by total surrender, loving trust, and cheerfulness.

OCTOBER 29

Prayer is a sacred duty and a sublime mission. We ascend the altar of prayer, conscious of the many urgent needs and interests of others, taking up our rosary, embracing all the other spiritual exercises with great longing. We go with confidence to the throne of grace to obtain mercy and seasonable aid for ourselves and for souls.

OCTOBER 30

Wire can be bundled up—small and big, new and old, cheap and expensive—but unless the current passes through, there is no light. That wire is just like you and me. Our Lady was the most wonderful wire! She surrendered completely to God, became full of grace, and the current—the grace of God—flowed through her. The moment she was filled with this current, she went to Elizabeth's house to connect that other wire—John—to the current—Jesus. And Elizabeth said, "This child leapt with joy in my womb at your voice."

Let us ask Mary to help make that current within us so that Jesus can use us around the world to connect the hearts of men with the current, Jesus.

OCTOBER 31

After the fall of the Ethiopian emperor, most of the religious orders working in that country were asked to leave. The military regime that followed told Mother Teresa's sisters: "We will not send you away because you love our people."

As Mother Teresa was visiting General Mengistu Haile Mariam, to thank him for his permission to stay, the general asked if he could do anything for her while she was in Ethiopia. Mother said, "Yes, I would like to visit the women of the emperor's family who are in prison."

The general, surprised by the request, became very stiff in a military reaction. He replied, "What courage, Mother; they are the enemy of the state." Mother said, "They were my friends and they still are, so I have, as you say, the courage of asking to see them." After this she was allowed to visit the prison and bring some relief to them.

November 1

On All Saints Day we pray to those who are where we want to go, and on All Souls Day we pray for those still suffering in purgatory and far from God.

November 2

For the month of Holy Souls and in union with their silence, let us offer to God many acts of silence. We must be extremely kind and gentle when helping the dying. Let us make the mercy of God very real to help the dying person turn to God with great confidence.

November 3

If you were to die today, what would others say about you? What was in you that was beautiful, that was Christlike, that helped others to pray better? Face yourself, with Jesus at your side, and do not be satisfied with just any answer.

NOVEMBER 4

If we earnestly desire holiness, three things are necessary: Prayer, self-denial, and charity. We must pray fervently and with the utmost fidelity. We must deny ourselves by controlling our bodily sense—the easiest form of self-denial—and by practicing interior mortifications and bodily penances. We must develop a spirit of fraternal charity, which requires humility on our part, a realization of our nothingness, and God's grace. We must have gratitude in our souls.

With St. Paul, we say: "I give no thought to what lies behind but push on to what is ahead. My entire attention is on the finish line as I run toward the prize to which God calls me—life on high in Christ Jesus."

NOVEMBER 5

Do not let anything take you away from the work of the dying destitute at Nirmal Hriday and the lepers. Our love for Jesus is poured out in action through these humble works. Like Mary, let us never be ashamed to do humble work. Like her, let us always accept the cross in whatever way it comes.

Humility of the heart of Mary, fill my heart. Teach me, as you taught Jesus, to be meek and humble and so to glorify the Father.

NOVEMBER 6

I am so used to seeing the smile of our poor people, even the dying ones smile.

NOVEMBER 7

What joy is ours that through our works of charity we are always in close contact with Christ in his distressing disguise of the poor. We fulfill the gospel. Jesus said that "you did it to me" when we serve the hungry, the thirsty, the naked, the homeless, the unwanted, the untouchable. How great is our calling! How fortunate people would think themselves if they were given the chance to give personal service to the king of this world. And here we are, able to touch, love, and care for Christ all the days of our lives.

NOVEMBER 8

Our work is not a profession but a vocation, chosen to satiate the thirst of Jesus by total surrender, complete, without counting the cost.

NOVEMBER 9

I met a couple in Bangladesh. When the wife died, her husband, being overwhelmed by grief, wrote to me. I wrote back to him, "Your wife was loving, she had a big heart for the suffering, and she went to Jesus. Since Jesus is in your heart, she must be there too, more close than before."

NOVEMBER 10

You might be doing great good somewhere but if you are sent elsewhere, you must be ready to leave. The work belongs to Jesus, not to us. Obedience and humility are the same thing. If you want to know if you are humble, ask yourself: "Do I obey because I see Christ in every command?" You can get used to poverty, but every act of obedience is an act of the will. It gets harder as we get older because we have our own ideas and resent advice and interference. Ask the Holy Spirit to give you the grace of obedience.

NOVEMBER 11

To bring joy to us, Jesus became man.

Are we convinced of Christ's love for us and our love for him? This conviction is like the sunlight which makes the sap of life rise and the buds of sanctity bloom. This conviction is the rock on which sanctity is built. To have this conviction we must know Jesus, love Jesus, and serve Jesus. We know him through prayers, meditations, and spiritual duties. We love him through Mass and the sacraments and our intimate union with him. We serve him under the distressing disguise of the poorest of the poor and everyone we meet.

Today is the feast of St. Stanislaus. St. Stanislaus was a novice, a young soul with a big heart. He had in his heart one love for the purity of Mary and a real personal love for the Bread of Life: Jesus in the Eucharist.

He loved the purity of Our Lady so much that he wanted to be pure as she, so that he, too, could receive Jesus as she received Jesus.

What helped St. Stanislaus to become holy were those little things he kept faithful to: silence of the eyes, silence of the mouth, silence of the ears, silence of the mind, and silence of the heart.

NOVEMBER 14

We must make ourselves attractive to God, like Our Lady. Holiness is a normal thing, nothing extraordinary.

NOVEMBER 15

Socrates, a pagan philosopher, used to go down the street, look around, and say, "I need none of these things." He was not a Christian and he did not know Jesus, he did not take a vow of poverty, yet he chose to give up and not to be attached to anything.

NOVEMBER 16

Give your heart to God, deliberately, knowingly, willingly. It belongs to him.

As the poor continue to grow poorer, let us be more cheerful about the poverty of our own houses. The poor are denied so many of the daily necessities of life. Let us be more careful of our use of these things so that we may share their hardship in obtaining food, clothing, water, soap, and electricity.

Pray to know the will of God and to accept the will of God. We should do his will with obedience. Jesus did the will of his Father unto death on the cross. Mary chose obedience when she said, "Be it done unto me according to your word." This obedience is the surest way to true holiness.

Remember that Jesus said, "When you did it for one of my least brothers, you did it for me." We are holy because we touch the body of Jesus twenty-four hours a day.

Our Lady will help us to live in Jesus, with him, and for him. Jesus will be our sole guide and we will be invaded by his own holiness, filled with his own spirit of love. Do all for Jesus and be like Mary, filled with Jesus.

NOVEMBER 20

In most of the places we live, our presence has created a concern for and an awareness of the poor. More than ever, people want to see love in action through humble works. It is necessary for us to be in love with Jesus, to be able to feed him in the hungry and lonely.

NOVEMBER 21

Once a girl who was crippled and retarded came to Shishu Bhavan. When she came to the church and saw the bread, cross, and host, she pointed to bread and mouth, the host and cross. She understood more than any theologian.

NOVEMBER 22

Obedience makes us most like Jesus and one with him. If we really obey, it is a constant crucifixion.

We forget, sometimes, that we are called to give God's love and compassion first to our families, those who are the very life of our life. So often, in our heart, there is bitterness; on our tongue, there are ugly words; in our attitude, there is pride. To think that in that very heart Jesus comes; so on that very tongue we receive Jesus; and that attitude is so unworthy of us who are called to belong to Christ.

NOVEMBER 24

Advent is like springtime in nature when everything is renewed, fresh, and healthy. Advent refreshes us, makes us healthy and able to receive Christ in whatever form he may come to us. At Christmas, he comes as a little child, small, helpless, and in need of his mother and all that a mother's love can give. His mother's humility enabled her to serve. If we really want God to fill us, we must empty ourselves through humility of all the selfishness within us.

NOVEMBER 25

Of our own free will, we have chosen to be faithful to poverty. This poverty is a sign of God, of the true poverty of Christ. Radiate the joy of being poor, not telling people of our hard life but just being happy to be poor with Christ.

November 26

The best way to show gratitude to God and to others is to accept everything with joy. One day, people brought us a man from the streets. After we had washed him and given him a ticket to St. Peter, he said, "Sisters, I am going to God."

That is joy.

November 27

Nothing will destroy our joy of loving Jesus as much as money. It is one of the keys of the devil that will open any heart. It is the beginning of great evil.

November 28

Our works of love are nothing but works of peace. Let us do these works with great love in our daily life, in the home, for our neighbor.

Christ says:

I was hungry, not only for food but for peace that comes from a pure heart.

I was thirsty, not for water but for peace that comes from freedom from war.

I was naked, not for clothes but for dignity.

I was homeless, not for a shelter made of bricks but for a heart that understands, that covers, that loves.

Eternal God, your eyes are upon all your works, especially intent on your servants. Turn away from us whatever is hurtful and grant us whatever is advantageous, that through your favor and under the benign influence of your special Providence, we may securely pass through the transitory dangers and difficulties of this life and happily arrive at the eternal joys of the next, through Christ our Lord. Amen.

NOVEMBER 30

In 1994, Mother Teresa M.C. was the featured speaker at the National Prayer Breakfast in Washington, D.C. President Bill Clinton attended. This meeting was one which made history.

The tiny, frail nun from Calcutta spoke powerful words in defense of the unborn. She said, "At our children's home in Calcutta alone, we have saved over three thousand children from abortion. These children have brought so much love and joy to their adoptive parents and have grown up so full of love and joy. Please don't kill the child. I want the child. I am willing to accept any child who would be aborted and give him or her to a married couple who would love the child and be loved by the child.

Mother told me later, "After the meeting everyone stood up to show solidarity with my words; only the president reached for a glass of water."

DECEMBER 1

Heavenly Father, you have given us a model of life in the Holy Family of Nazareth. Help us, O loving Father, to make our family another Nazareth where love, peace, and joy reign. May it be deeply contemplative, intensely eucharistic, and vibrant with joy.

Help us to stay together in joy and sorrow through family prayer.

Teach us to see Jesus in the members of our family, especially in their distressing disguise.

May the eucharistic heart of Jesus make our hearts meek and humble like his and help us to carry out our family duties in a holy way.

May we love one another as God loves each one of us more and more each day, and forgive each others' faults as you forgive our sins.

Help us, O loving Father, to take whatever you give and to give whatever you take with a big smile.

Immaculate Heart of Mary, cause of our joy, pray for us.

St. Joseph, pray for us.

Holy Guardian Angels, be always with us, guide and protect us. Amen.

In preparation for the coming of Jesus, we place an empty crib in all our chapels. This year, let us prepare a better crib, one of humility, poverty, and the simplicity of the gospel. We need the simplicity of the life of Bethlehem and Nazareth in order to live the life of Calvary. Keep things simple and do not introduce things that don't fit with our way of life.

Remember that you are special to him; he has chosen you with great love. You may wonder why he chose you and not another. Maybe someone else could have done a better job than you or I. I think God wants to prove his greatness by using nothingness.

Much disorder has come into the world through the neglect of family prayer and prayer in religious communities. Such neglect may destroy holiness, the very fruit of prayer. Jesus said, "Where two or three are gathered in my name, there am I in the midst of them." The Holy Spirit came upon the disciples when they were together in prayer with Mary. Fidelity to prayer is the beginning of holiness.

DECEMBER 4

Jesus wants us to prepare the way for his coming, for there are so many blocks in the way of his becoming all in all for us. Give him whatever he takes and take from him whatever he gives with a big smile.

Be a cause of joy to others.

Speak well of everybody.

Smile at all you meet.

Deliberately make three acts of loving kindness every day.

Confess any sin against charity.

If you offend anyone—even a small child—ask forgiveness before going to bed.

Read about, meditate on, and speak of this love.

DECEMBER 5

Greet the children, the poor, the suffering, the lonely with a happy smile. Give them not only your care but also your heart. Kindness has converted more people than zeal or eloquence. Our service to others should be kind, sweet, humble, unspoiled by selfishness. Let no one ever come to you without coming away better and happier. Be the living expression of God's kindness.

DECEMBER 6

Frequently schoolteachers came to the mother-house in Calcutta to visit Mother while seeking a moment of closeness with God. Two of them, a Hindu couple, asked Mother Teresa this question, "Mother, tell us something to make us better husband and wife." Mother Teresa replied with her wit, "Smile at each other." The wife thought for a moment and asked, "Are you married?" Mother Teresa replied, "Yes, and sometimes I find it very difficult to smile at Jesus, my husband, because he can be very demanding."

DECEMBER 7

The good God has given himself to us in order to bring joy into our very soul.

In Bethlehem, the angel announced tidings of great joy. Jesus wanted to share his joy with his apostles and prayed that "my joy may be yours." Joy was the password of the first Christians. In various ways, St. Paul repeats the refrain of joy: "Rejoice in the Lord always, again I say, rejoice."

In return for the great grace of baptism, may you serve the church joyfully. And remember, joy is not simply a matter of temperament, but of choice; it must be cultivated.

DECEMBER 8

On this feast of the Immaculate Conception, let us consecrate our lives to Mary. Through her guidance, each of us can become the spouse of Jesus crucified. How clean our words must be to be able to proclaim the good news to the poor. Mary, the most pure virgin, will teach us to be pure so that when the poor look at us they see only Jesus.

DECEMBER 9

Very often, small misunderstandings—repeated over and over—become the cause of so much suffering. Bring love to all you do and you will fulfill your vocation.

DECEMBER 10

Love, in order to be true, must hurt. God loved the world so much that he gave his Son. His Son loved the world so much that he gave his life. He asks us to love as he loved, by giving ourselves.

In a gospel play, amongst the people of the slums, a child had to take the part of the innkeeper. This child had to say, "Sorry, there is no room in the inn." He said, "I cannot say that to St. Joseph." The sister explained to him that it was only a play so the child agreed. When the time came and the child had to do his part, he said: "There's no room in the inn but if you'd like a drink, come in."

The angel Gabriel and St. Joseph the carpenter were instruments of God's will for Mary. She responded with prompt obedience. If we accept with humility and joy the message of God spoken to us through our superiors, we, too, will become pleasing to God and carriers of his love.

December 13

Let us ask Our Lady and St. Joseph to make our families what their family was for Jesus at Nazareth. Love does not live on words nor can it be explained by words. This is especially true of that love that is in Jesus and comes from Jesus and finds Jesus—touches him, serves him, loves him—in others. Such love is true, burning, pure, free from fear and doubt. There is no greater love than the love Christ himself has shown us. We must love one another with the same love.

December 14

We look but we don't see. Some time ago a woman came to me with her child and said, "Mother, I went to several places to beg for some food, for we have not eaten for three days, but I was told that I am young and I must work if I want to eat, and no one gave me anything."

I immediately went to get some food, but by the time I returned the baby in her arms had died of hunger.

DECEMBER 15

The thoughtfulness of Jesus, Mary, and Joseph was so great that it made Nazareth the abode of the Most High. If we have that thoughtfulness for each other, our homes will really become the abode of God, Most High. The quickest and surest way to that goal is to tame the tongue, using it to speak well of others. From the abundance of the heart, the mouth speaks. If your heart is full of love, you will speak of love.

DECEMBER 16

If Mary and Joseph were looking for a place to make a home for Jesus, would they choose our home? In our community, does our life of poverty resemble that of the manger at Bethlehem? During this season of Advent, let us meditate on poverty so that we might love it and live it. To experience the joy and freedom of poverty as Jesus did we need the surrender of obedience, for that is the foundation of his love.

December 17

Today, we see that all the suffering in the world has started from the home. Today, we have not time even to look at each other, to talk to each other, to enjoy each other, and still less to be what our children expect from us, what the husband expects from the wife, what the wife expects from the husband. And so more and more we are homeless at home because less and less we are in touch with each other.

December 18

Poverty is joy. We must be happy with what we have and be happy with what we don't have. Poverty for us is a choice and therefore a joy. The less we have the more we can give.

December 19

We are called to live the love of God, not to feel the love of God. We live this love through prayer and action. Our work is the fruit of our prayer, so that if our work is not going well, we must examine our prayer life. If we neglect our work or are harsh, proud, moody, and angry, then we should examine our prayer life. We will see that something has gone wrong there.

Radiate and live the life of Christ. Be an angel of comfort to a sick friend. Be a friend to little children. Love others as God loves each of us, with a special, intense love. Be kind to each other, speak kindly to each other. It is better to make a mistake while acting kindly than to work a miracle while acting unkindly.

At Christmas, may you be filled with the joy, love, and peace of Jesus, newly formed within you and around you. Christ comes at Christmas as a little child, small, helpless, so much in need of all that love can give. Are you ready to receive him? His parents looked for a simple dwelling place for his birth but there was none. If they came to you in search of a home, would they choose your heart and all that it holds?

The birthday of Jesus is coming very near.
Jesus is the light,
Jesus is the truth,
Jesus is the life.
We, too, must be the light of charity, the truth of humility, and the life of sanctity.

DECEMBER 23

God loves the world so much—that is, you and me. He doesn't love riches or greatness, he didn't come to dwell in a palace. No, when he came into the world he became so very small—he became a child, born to a virgin, placed in a manger. Mary did not expect him to be born in this humble way. This seems so strange that we must stop and ask ourselves why he did this. Jesus could have had wealth; instead, he chose poverty. I think poverty must be seen as beautiful in heaven if Jesus would choose to become so small, so poor.

To understand the poor, we must know what poverty is and why Jesus made himself poor. If we understand our poverty, our smallness, our weakness, our littleness, then we will be able to serve the poor and give Christ to the poor.

DECEMBER 24

I received a strange letter from a Hindu man. One Christmas night while walking down the street, he saw a mother with a piece of white cloth and a few flowers around it. It was a dead child, a child who was not given a chance to live and love.

He connected Bethlehem and the little child and he realized that through that little child he was facing the message of Bethlehem.

Hail and blessed be the hour and moment in which the Son of God was born of the most pure virgin Mary at midnight in Bethlehem, in piercing cold. In that hour vouchsafe, O my God, to hear our prayers and grant our desires, through the merits of our savior, Jesus Christ, and his blessed Mother. Amen.

DECEMBER 26

Christmastime shows us how small God made himself. Go to the crib and see how small he became, how he lived that total surrender to the full.

We must learn to be that child in complete surrender and trust and joy.

See the joy of the child Jesus and the joy of Christmas! Never be moody, never let anything take away that joy. Christmas shows us how much heaven appreciates humility, surrender, poverty, because God himself, who made you and me, became so small, so poor, so humble.

DECEMBER 27

St. John said, "How can you say that you love God whom you do not see, when you do not love your neighbor whom you do see?" He uses a very strong word. He says, "You are a liar if you say you love God and you don't love your neighbor." I think this is something we must all understand, that love begins at home.

DECEMBER 28

Every day I pray, please let my people grow in holiness. You must surrender yourselves completely to God and pray for each other. You must be really holy. I need holy people to offer to God. I don't need numbers, I need real Missionaries of Charity to offer to God as a sacrifice. You must fulfill the promise Mother made to give saints to mother church. Take this as an obligation, take it seriously.

DECEMBER 29

As Missionaries of Charity, we stand before the world as ambassadors of peace. We preach a message of love in action that crosses all barriers of nationality and creed. The Holy Father has said that vocation today means preferring the inner to the external life. It means choosing an austere and constant perfection instead of comfortable and insignificant mediocrity. Our vocation is truly great because it demands so much from us, calling us to overtake Christ. What does it profit a man to follow Christ if he fails to overtake him?

DECEMBER 30

The following quotation is taken from the last general letter Mother Teresa wrote on the day of her death:

"Let our gratitude be our strong resolution to quench the thirst of Jesus by lives of real charity. Love for Jesus in prayer, love for Jesus in your brothers and sisters, love for Jesus in the poorest of the poor. Nothing else."

DECEMBER 31

This message brings you Mother's prayers and God's special blessing on each one of you during this past year. As we come to the end of these 365 days, it is good that we look at the beautiful things God has done for us, with us, and through us.

For the grace of perseverance up to today;

for the acceptance of our poor, for giving us their love and trust;

for the people who have shared the work with their hearts, hands, and all sorts of help.

Thank you does not express what I would like to say, so let me tell you that my gratitude to you is my prayer for you.

Let us thank Jesus for all these gifts and promise that we will make our society something beautiful for God.

EPILOGUE

J.M.J.

New York. 10/9/96

Dear members of the third Order
of the Missionaries of Charity.
"Universal Fraternity of the Word."
You are the Gift of God for the Golden
Jubelee of the "Inspiration Day" which gave
birth to our Society. The Missionaries of
Charity. "Be one heart full of love" Ek dil
prem pur" God will take care of you and
multiply you. if you remain one. All
for Jesus through Mary. Let us pray.

God bless you
Mc Teresa mc.

STATUTES OF THE THIRD ORDER OF THE
MISSIONARIES OF CHARITY
"UNIVERSAL FRATERNITY
OF THE WORD"
M.C.III.O.

Article 1: NAME AND STATUS IN THE CHURCH

The third order of the Missionaries of Charity "Universal Fraternity of the Word," is a private association of Christian faithful and a movement of new evangelization which has the same aim and spirit as the Missionaries of Charity. It was co-founded by Mother Teresa of Calcutta and Fr. Angelo Devananda Scolozzi, her collaborator in this service.

This third order is a branch of the Missionaries of Charity, and completes Mother Teresa's missionary work by offering to the laity the opportunity to share in the task of the "New Evangelization" of the world's spiritually poorest of the poor, at the approach of the third millennium. By its universal character, our Association partakes of "the special mission of the Church, which is to spread the light of the gospel message throughout the world, and to unify under one Spirit, all people from any country, race, and culture, being a sign of that universal brotherhood that fosters and supports an honest dialogue" (Cf. GS. 932). As a third order and a private association of Christian faithful, we are governed by the specific norms of canon law regarding such associations (Cf. canon 303 and 321-29).

Article 2: SPIRIT

Having for our ideal no one but Christ, the spirit of the Association is one of loving trust, total surrender, and cheerfulness, as lived by the Holy Family at Nazareth.

Article 3: GENERAL AIM

Our aim is to quench the infinite thirst of Jesus Christ agonizing on the cross for love of souls through a life inspired by the promises of the evangelical counsels and wholehearted free service to the spiritually poorest of the poor, lived in keeping with each one's state of life, according to the statutes of the Universal Fraternity of the Word. Such promises are called "*DEDICATION.*" Their observance leads each one of us toward the perfect love of God and our neighbor, which is the realization of his kingdom on earth and makes the church fully present in the world today (Cf. GS.85).

The greatest desire of Jesus at the Last Supper was "that they all be one so that the world may believe" (Jn 17:21), and because "interreligious dialogue is also a part of the church's evangelizing mission" (AAS 83-91.302), we ardently desire through our Association to be a means of reunification for all

Christians and, as carriers of God's love, of spiritual awakening for all humankind.

Article 4: PARTICULAR MISSION

Our particular mission is to labor at the salvation and sanctification of the spiritually poorest of the poor, in ourselves, in our families, in our Fraternity, and all over the world by:

Knowing the Word of God in reading, meditation, prayer, and study of the Scriptures.

Loving the Word of God disguised in bread and wine to nourish our spiritual hunger by fervent celebration of the Eucharist and by adoration.

Living the Word of God in process of conversion and purity of heart, renouncing the way of the world in a constant renewal of the grace of our baptism and confirmation. We simplify our lifestyle according to humility of the gospel so as to be nearer to the people we evangelize and serve.

Speaking the Word of God to all people and to the spiritually poorest of the poor in whose distressing disguise Christ Jesus himself is present, starting with our own families. Such proclamation of the gospel of salvation will be carried out individual to individual, family to family, parish to parish, diocese to diocese. We shall start with the territory most dechristianized, in a movement of new evangelization and spiritual renewal to the remotest corners of the earth, according to Christ's command, as we await his last manifestation and glorious return. This evangelical life of study, prayer, and service will be our specific call to proclaim to all nations that "Jesus is Lord."

Article 5: OUR PATRONS
Our association is dedicated to the Holy Family of Nazareth and especially to Mary, First Carrier of the Word.

Article 6: APOSTOLATE
For the concrete realization of our ideal we shall establish, administer, and direct retreat programs, groups of prayer, houses of prayer, and places of welcome for moral rehabilitation which are to be true schools of life and recovery. These houses are for everyone regardless of race, class, creed, or culture. They are open for those who, feeling conflict with themselves, are rejected, unloved, broken in their lives and their spirits, and being spiritually poor, are looking for the Word of Life to evangelize and comfort them, and for a friendly hand to guide them. We will have particular care for those who, at the margins of society, abandoned to themselves, are exposed and fall victims to a world of new paganism, which is competitive, materialistic, and devoid of authentic spiritual values.

The fruitfulness of our work will not depend on the availability of particularly important means, but on our being rooted in Christ and on our deliberate choice of rendering simple and humble services with great love.

Article 7: ASSOCIATES

As the Association is, and will be, what its members make it, great care and prudence must be exercised in admitting candidates desirous to lead our way of life. There are several stages to the membership of the community. The Universal Brothers and Sisters of the Word can be members who are *CO-OPERATORS, TEMPORARILY DEDICATED,* or *PERPETUALLY DEDICATED.*

A *simple affiliation* is offered to individuals and families in special situations.

CO-OPERATORS. The "Co-operators" are simple Christians wishing to be the seed of a "new evangelization." They participate in group prayer, in the study of Scriptures, and in catechesis on the fundamentals. They frequent the sacraments, attend Sunday Mass together with their families, and strive to live evangelically according to the Sermon on the Mount in order to convert from worldly ways. They make a yearly retreat, remain in their families, retain their own occupation, and stay within the framework of their churches. A period of "come and see" must precede the formal acceptance into the membership which is made preferentially on the feast day of the Holy Family.

TEMPORARILY DEDICATED. Christians, men or women, who desire to "dedicate" their lives in a more committed way to God and to the gospel, according to the aims and activities of the

Association, may do so by "dedicating" themselves with temporary promises, that is, one year at a time. If they are married they remain with their families. Before committing themselves in this deeper way, they must undergo two years of formation under the Servant Leader or under some other qualified member appointed by him. If they are married they must obtain the consent of their families before beginning this formation. The "Temporary Dedication" is normally made on the feasts of the Annunciation or the Visitation of Our Lady.

PERPETUALLY DEDICATED. Brothers or Sisters who are already "Temporarily Dedicated," be they single or married, moved by a desire to consecrate all aspects of their lives to God within the Association, may, after several years of training, ask to be admitted to "Perpetual Dedication." Single "Perpetually Dedicated" members may live in a community of single Brothers or of single Sisters. A married person requires the participation of the spouse in such a "Dedication." "Perpetually Dedicated" married members may live with their families according to their lay state or may choose, along with their families, to live in the proximity of a community of single Brothers or Sisters to the extent possible to them. The purpose of living a community life is to witness among ourselves, and to the world, the truth and values of the gospel just as the first Christians experienced and radiated the living presence of Jesus and his Spirit among themselves (see Acts 2:42-47) (Cf.

PC. 15). The "Perpetual Dedication" is normally made on the Feast of Pentecost.

Deacons and priests, willing to share our way of life, with the consent of their bishops, can join our association. They may remain in the framework of their diocese, or if permitted to do so may join us in our community living. Members of our association wishing to be candidates to the permanent diaconate and priesthood will be trained in diocesan or pontifical seminaries until a place of formation appropriate to the spirituality of our association can be established for them. In this we must be attentive to the needs of both the universal and the local church.

AFFILIATION
Individuals or families of other Christian denominations, or of other religions, are also welcome to participate in the life and in the spirit of the fraternity, as far as they are able. This will be a "Simple Affiliation" for people desiring to take part in our fellowship but who are limited in their ability to do so.

Article 8: GOVERNMENT
The government of the Association is composed of:
    a) The Assembly of the Brothers and Sisters;
    b) The General Council;
    c) The Servant General, also called the Servant Leader.

Article 9: ASSEMBLY

The Assembly is composed of all the "Perpetually Dedicated" Brothers and Sisters present in person or by delegation. It is the supreme governing body of the Association, and it is ordinarily convoked every third year in the month of June. The purpose of this convocation is to assess the progress of the Association, to approve the Servant Leader's reports, and to examine the directions of the Association proposed by the Council. For serious reasons, the Assembly can be convoked to a special session by the decision of the General Council or by the request of the majority of the "Perpetually Dedicated" members.

Article 10: GENERAL COUNCIL

The General Council is composed of the Servant Leader and of two Councillors elected by the assembly. The Servant Leader must be confirmed by the competent ecclesiastical authority. The mandate of the General Council is for six years. The election of the Servant Leader can be reconfirmed at the discretion of the Assembly. The General Council meets twice a year and whenever the Servant Leader deems it fitting, or when it is requested by the majority of its members.

The General Council approves:

  a) The admission of the "Co-operators" and the "Temporarily Dedicated" Brothers and Sisters and their dismissal as a consequence of behavior seriously contrary to the spirit of the statutes or for failure to maintain active collaboration.

b) The undertaking of extraordinary administration.

c) The election of the Secretary General and the Procurator, from among the Councillors.

d) The directives of the Association to be submitted to the Assembly.

e) The approval of the financial accounts.

f) Whatever other decisions relating to the life of the Association that are not under the competence of any other body.

Article 11: THE SERVANT GENERAL OR SERVANT LEADER

a) He is the legal representative of the Association and directs it according to the Statutes, and convokes and presides over the Assembly and over the General Council.

b) The Servant Leader approves the admission to "Perpetual Dedication" of those Brothers and Sisters already "Temporarily Dedicated," and their dismissal for grave reasons.

c) He opens new houses having consulted the General Council.

d) If necessary, he may nominate one or two supplementary Councillors.

e) He takes care of the ordinary administration of the Association and draws up the annual budget reports.

f) In case there is no Servant Leader, the Secretary General assumes the functions "ad interim" and within three months, convokes the Assembly for the election of a substitute Servant Leader for the remainder of the current mandate.

Article 12: MEANS
The single "Perpetually Dedicated" Brothers or Sisters living in community may depend on Divine Providence with childlike trust for all their needs, material and spiritual. We shall neither raise funds nor allow others to raise funds for us, but we shall gratefully accept donations in cash or kind. All our services for the poorest of the poor will be wholehearted and free. All gifts received by the Association will be handled with great responsibility as trustees. We shall be mindful of the donor's intentions and give an exact account of the money received and spent.

Article 13: AUDITORS OF ACCOUNTS
The accounts are drawn up by three auditors nominated by the Assembly. They may be selected from persons outside the Association and preferably chosen from professionals of outstanding honesty and competence. Their term lasts for three years and they can be reappointed.

Article 14: DISSOLUTION
In case the Association is dissolved, the assets will accrue to the Congregation of the Missionaries of Charity Sisters.

Article 15: DIRECTORY

Of special spiritual value is the fraternity directory, "Alliance of Life," for the implementation of the present Statutes, in which we are able to recognize the light of the special charisma we have received through our foundress Mother Teresa M.C. of Calcutta, for the good of the church among the spiritually poorest of the poor.

Article 16: STATUTES MODIFICATION

The present Statutes can be modified by the Assembly's proposal when 75 percent of the "Perpetually Dedicated" Brothers and Sisters are present, personally or by proxy, and when approved by the competent ecclesiastical authority.

Article 17: CONCLUSION

In the case of anything for which provision is not made in the present Statutes, the norms of canon law and civil law of the country in which we are living must be observed.

Calcutta 1ˢᵗ May 1996:
Feast of St. Joseph the Worker,
Patron of the Universal Church.

Let it all be for Revised
the Glory of God and 31st May 1996
the Good of Souls God bless you
Let us pray lu Teresa mc
Mc Teresa mc

Witness:
Sr. Sy. Frederick H.C.
M. Nirmala M L   fr. angelo Devananda Sioloski M.C.III.O.

If you enjoyed *Thirsting for God: A Yearbook of Prayers, Meditations, and Anecdotes*, we highly recommend the following books:

No Greater Love

Destined to be a spiritual classic, this elegant volume is the most accessible and inspiring collection of Mother Teresa's teachings ever published. hardcover, 224 pages. Published by New World Library

In the Heart of the World

A powerful portrait of one of the most beloved women of all time, told in her own words through a fascinating blend of daily life experiences, prayers, and spiritual wisdom. With humor, compassion, and clarity, Mother Teresa illuminates the sacred in the intimate everyday tasks of living. 112 pages. Published by New World Library.

APPENDIX

"Cooperation and Simple Affiliation" To the Missionaries of Charity Third Order

There are several stages of membership to the M.C.III.O.

"Cooperators" are simple Christians wishing to be the seeds of a "new evangelization" as we enter the third millennium. They participate in a group that meets for prayer, the study of the scriptures and catechesis about the basics of our Christian faith.

They remain in their families, retain their secular occupations, worship and function in the framework of their churches and parishes.

A six month period of "Come and see" (John 1:39) normally precedes formal acceptance into the M.C.III.O.

The servant leader of the association or his delegate makes this formal acceptance, preferentially but not exclusively, during the Feast of the Holy Family which is held on the first Sunday following Christmas.

A request to the servant leader of the M.C.III.O. that an individual or a group of individuals intend to start the "Come and see..." period is sufficient.

"Simple Affiliation" is offered to individuals, families, or groups of other Christian denominations, or of other religious wishing to participate in the life and spirit of the association. Knowing that their ability to do so will be limited by cultural and religious boundaries, it is important to determine their role in the M.C.III.O. At the proper times, the servant leader will discern the way to proceed the participation for each group of affiliates.

FORMAT FOR THE M.C.III.O.

Meetings

1. Contact a friend or two interested in starting a M.C.III.O. group with you and request, by writing to us, that an information package be sent to you.

2. Seek permission from your pastor to put leaflets about the M.C.III.O. in the back of your church or, if you prefer, put an announcement in your parish bulletin, your diocesan paper or in some other local publication. Include the date, time, place and purpose of your meeting.

3. Select a suitable place for the meeting. It could be a church, a temple, a synagogue, a school room, a college cafeteria, a nursing home, a hospital, a prison, a front store room, a home, etc.

4. Start the meeting by introducing yourself and greeting each other. Have a spontaneous prayer in which everyone could participate. You would then recite or sing a hymn to the Holy Spirit or some other appropriate song. A particular group may choose to have a brief period of adoration, recite part of the divine office, morning or evening of the Christian prayer, or may say a rosary or a simple decade of the rosary.

5. Following the initial moment of prayer, have a pre-selected passage from the Scriptures; it could be the liturgical readings of the following Sunday from your missalette, or start with the book of the "Acts of the Apostles" which relates to the beginning of the Christian community. Each one taking turns to read a few verses at a time.

6. After the reading of the Scriptures and a moment of reflective silence, a practical application of the Word to our daily living should be made by various participants; a kind of faith sharing and witnessing or life story giving. A time suitable to foster the bond of charity where people would befriend each other which is, as Mother Teresa said, the first step of evangelization. A litanic prayer of petitions would be proper now: Let us pray for various intentions ... ending with the "Our Father."

7. After this, a short, optional, coffee break could be made and the group should then proceed to reading a daily passage from Mother Teresa's spiritual doctrine and an article of the statutes which

are in the back of this book, or in the 1998 new edition of *Jesus the Word to Be Spoken,* published by Servant Publications.

8.Before concluding, a person appointed by common consent should be chosen to be the local servant leader of the group and a date, time, place and agenda of the next group meeting should be agreed upon.

9.The local servant leader for the group of collaborators or for the group of affiliates has the task of:

Keeping contact with the other members of the group, reminding them if necessary of the date, time, and place of the meetings.

Moderate the process of the meeting insuring that it would be opened and closed in time according to the length previously agreed upon. See that someone would be there to substitute for him/her if they must be absent on occasions.

Foster wholehearted free service or charitable activity among the members of the group toward the spiritually or materially poorest in the community according to the local needs and circumstances.

Write a quarterly report about the life of the group and send it to the central place of the association in Cleveland, TX so that news from every group could be periodically shared in the common bulletin of the M.C.III.O.: "I Thirst"

10.As a conclusion of the group, the universal prayer of St. Francis with the one composed by Pope Paul the VI and Mother Teresa for the M.C. society will be said by all.

Mother Teresa's vision of a new evangelization of the world, as we enter the new millennium, would not be possible without your free, spontaneous and joyous participation. She wrote in her very last message, the day of her death, "Loving trust and total surrender made Our Lady say 'yes' to the message of the angel and cheerfulness made her run in haste to serve her cousin Elizabeth. That is so much our life—saying 'yes' to Jesus and running in haste to serve Him in the poorest of the poor."

"Today, if you listen to his voice, harden not your heart" (Ps 95:8).

You could make a difference in the creation of a better world if you are willing; you have the "power of one"! It would be only a drop in the ocean but, according to Mother, the ocean would be a drop less without your free participation. Just one person at a time, a day at a time, doing little things with great love…. If not you, who? If not today, when? For me and you, let it be now. Marantha. Come Lord Jesus.

Universal Prayer for Peace
by St. Francis of Assisi

Lord, make me a channel of your peace,
That where there is hatred,
I may bring love;
Where there is wrong,
I may bring the spirit of forgiveness;
Where there is discord,
I may bring harmony;
Where there is error,
I may bring truth;
Where there is doubt,
I may bring faith;
Where there is despair,
I may bring hope;
Where there are shadows,
I may bring light;
Where there is sadness,
I may bring joy.
Lord, grant that I may seek rather to
comfort than to be comforted;
To understand than to be understood;
To love than to be loved;
For it is by forgetting self that one finds.
It is by forgiving that one is forgiven.
It is in dying that one awakens into eternal life. Amen.

Prayer of Pope Paul VI and Mother Teresa M.C.

Make us worthy, Lord, to serve our
fellow men throughout the world who
live and die in poverty and hunger.
Give them through our hands, this day
their daily bread, and by our understanding
love give peace and joy.

Immaculate heart of Mary, cause of our joy,
Bless your own Missionaries of Charity.
Help us to do all the good we can.
Keep us in your most pure heart.
So that we may please Jesus
Through you, in you and with you.
Mary, First Carrier of the Word, pray for us.

For more information about the
Missionaries of Charity Third Order M.C.III.O.,
please write:

Missionaries of Charity
736 Cheltenham Drive
El Paso, TX 79912-1530
Phone: 915-581-7277